Tort Law in South Korea

Tort Law in South Korea

Sang Joong Kim
Seil Ko

This book was originally published as a monograph in the International Encyclopaedia of Laws/Tort Law.

Founding Editor: Roger Blanpain
General Editor: Frank Hendrickx
Volume Editor: Britt Weyts

Wolters Kluwer

Published by:
Kluwer Law International B.V.
PO Box 316
2400 AH Alphen aan den Rijn
The Netherlands
E-mail: lrs-sales@wolterskluwer.com
Website: www.wolterskluwer.com/en/solutions/kluwerlawinternational

Sold and distributed by:
Wolters Kluwer Legal & Regulatory U.S.
920 Links Avenue
Landisville, PA 17538
United States of America
E-mail: customer.service@wolterskluwer.com

ISBN 978-94-035-0279-3

e-Book: ISBN 978-94-035-0289-2
web-PDF: ISBN 978-94-035-0299-1

This title is available on www.kluwerlawonline.com

The Authors

Sang Joong Kim is a professor of Civil Law at Korea University (South Korea). He has published in the fields of contracts, torts and has contributed to several commentaries on civil law (agency, breach of contract, tort). Recently, he has been interested in civil law issues related to privacy, data, platforms, and artificial intelligence and has written monographs and books on these areas. He received an LLB (1992) and LLM (1995) from Korea University. He went to Germany to study Civil Law and received Ph.D. (2003) from the University of Cologne (Germany).

Seil Ko is a professor of Civil Law at Chungnam National University (South Korea). He has published in the fields of contracts and torts. He has written many articles on American tort law. He was an editor-in-chief of artificial intelligence and law. Recently, he has been interested in Bible and Law and has studied this area. He received an LLB (1993) from Jeju National University an LLM (1996) from Korea University. He went to US to study American Law and received an LLM (2002) from University of Virginia and an LLM (2004) and Ph.D. (2007) from Tulane University. (U.S.A.). He has studied theology (M.Div.) at Fuller Seminary.

The Authors

Table of Contents

List of Abbreviations

APADR	The Act on Press Arbitration and Damages Remedies
CPA	Certified Public Accountant
GDP	Gross Domestic Product
USD	United Stated Dollars
PTDS	Post-Traumatic Stress Disorder
SME	Small and Medium Enterprise

List of Abbreviations

General Introduction

§1. THE GENERAL BACKGROUND OF THE COUNTRY

I. Geography

1. South Korea is located in the south-central part of the Korean Peninsula in the northeast of the Asian continent. The area of the Korean Peninsula is 181,035 km^2, of which the area of South Korea is 100,188.1 km^2. The Korean Peninsula borders China and Russia to the north, is surrounded by the sea on the other three sides and is adjacent to Japan across the sea. While the southern and western parts of Korea are largely plains, the eastern and northern parts are mountains. The capital of South Korea is Seoul.

2. As of December 31, 2021, the population of South Korea is 51,744,876, and the population density is 516.2 persons/km. In 2021, foreigners with Korean citizenship were 197,730.

There are 1,763,104 foreigners, including foreigners without Korean citizenship.[1] Most of the population speaks the Korean language.

II. History

3. The name Korea is derived from the Chinese name for Goryeo (Koryo) that succeeded Goguryeo. On the Korean Peninsula, Gojoseon, the first nation in the B.C.E., was bound.

After Gojoseon, there were three ancient Kingdoms period (Goguryeo, Baekje, and Silla), the medieval Goryeo (918–1392). After that, the era of the unified dynasty of the modern Joseon (1392–1897) continued. Until modern Western law in the late 19th century was accepted, traditional Korean law was influenced by religious norms such as Buddhism and Confucianism.

During this period, the public and criminal laws related to the organization, governance, and punishment of the state were mainly used. They were not distinguished from morals or ethics. At that time, public laws for organizing and

1. The above figures are based on statistical data stored in the Korean Statistical Information Service (https://kosis.kr/eng/).

controlling the organization of the State and criminal laws (e.g., Gyeongguk Daejeon compiled in 1455) were developed. However, the development of private law was sluggish.

4. Later, the Joseon dynasty was under strong pressure from internal social reform and external opening of the door. When Joseon was defeated by the imperialist powers, it was forced to open doors to trade and stopped its national isolation policy.

However, in 1876, the Treaty of Ganghwa Island was finally signed with Japan, and it later opened the door to the United States. It established diplomatic relations with Western powers. In the process, Joseon underwent two major social reforms: Kapohgyeongjang in 1894 and Eulmi Reform in 1895. Especially through Japan, Joseon accepted Western culture and systems. Thus, it had the chance to have modern laws of western societies. It could be accessible to the modern judicial system. Joseon found independence in the judiciary separate from the executive power, established a judiciary training center and learned modern law in the West.

In 1897, to have independent political and social reforms and to secure the sovereignty of the eroded nation, King Gojong changed from the nation of Joseon to the Korean Empire.

He became the first Korean emperor. The Korean Empire made and promulgated the constitution with the establishment of Korea, and the Criminal Law Code was compiled in 1905.

5. Korea was a Japanese colony until Japan was defeated in 1945 through the 1910 Korea-Japan Annexation Treaty. When Japan annexed Korea, it suppressed Joseon's independence movement and freedom of the press and the press. While depriving the Korean people of these fundamental rights, Japan made orders (the Jeryung) of the Governor-General of Joseon with respect to laws to be enforced in Korea. The most important law at that time, the Jeryung, was, in most cases, applied and governed by Japanese law. Thus, generally, in the case of civil matters, the civil and commercial laws of Japan were principally applied, unless otherwise stipulated by other laws. (Joseon Civil Order of 1912). Modern land ownership, ledger and registration system were also implemented during this period.

6. Korea was liberated from Japanese colonial rule in 1945 when Japan was defeated by the Allied Forces. But with the liberation, not only the left and right-wing powers were internally confronted but also the U.S. military and the Soviet Army occupied and separated South and North Korea, respectively, along the 38th parallel of the Korean peninsula.

In the case of South Korea, the U.S. military government began in September 1945, and the U.S. military government started abolition of evil laws enacted to strengthen Japan's colony rules and suppress Korean independence movements.

The U.S. military government established A Law Draft Foundation Committee in the judiciary to draft basic codes to replace the current Japanese laws concerning property rights, kinship, commercial relations, and punishment of crimes.

The U.S. military rule continued until 1948, during the time the Anglo-American Constitution and Human Rights Act could be accepted into Korean law.

7. In May 1948, as the United Nations resolved to hold a general election within the appropriate scope of the Korean Peninsula, the Republic of Korea, the Constituent Assembly was formed by holding general elections for the National Assembly members only in South Korea, which was under the control of the U.S. Military Government.

The Korean Constitution, which came into force on July 17, 1948, determined the form of government in the presidential system, and the National Assembly proclaimed that Syngmahn Rhee was elected South Korea's first president. In early days of Syngman Rhee, his government proceeded to seek modern land reform and the establishment of Western political order with the high public enthusiasm for modernization at the time. However, Syngman Rhee's regime suffered due to the long-term monopoly of power and arbitrary exercise of power. The government lost public support and finally a large-scale outbreak of the unlawful vice president election in 1960. It collided with student and citizen resistance and finally collapsed. Although modern social system and democratic constitutional order began during this period, the Korean War broke out in 1950. The Korean war lasted from 1950 to 1953, and it has had a huge influence on the divided South and North Korea.

8. In South Korea, the Syngman Rhee regime collapsed due to a large-scale student uprising in 1960 and a new democratic government emerged. However, the new government was unable to meet the democratic needs of the people at the time. Not only was it not enough to do so, but it was also struggling with factional conflicts. In this turmoil, Park Chung-hee organized a military coup with the military forces in May 1961. He dissolved the National Assembly and seized power. Even after the transfer of civil affairs from the military government, President Park Chung-hee, who was elected as a member of the government and maintained power since 1962, carried out economic development plans for industrialization and urbanization.

As a result, South Korea could achieve economic growth and social development in the 1970s. However, such state-led economic development was accompanied by repression of human and democratic rights, deepening social conflicts such as the gap between the rich and the poor, and strengthening of his political dictatorship. In 1979, Park Chung-hee was unexpectedly killed, leading to the end of the Park Chung-hee government. The country was once again faced with a political upheaval. However, even at that time, the military centered on Chun Doo-hwan.

The subordinate forces suppressed the desire for democratization at the time, which was once called the "Seoul Spring," and seized the political power. Meanwhile, the Chun Doo-hwan administration was conscious of the criticism of the past government, reinforced freedom and strengthened the rights of people, and maintained high economic growth under the favorable global economy at that time. Despite the economic growth, the government had the people's stigma of seizing power by force, which caused the people's resistance.

9. In South Korea, in 1987, the Chun Doo-hwan government intended to extend the anti-democratic regime at the end of his administration. However, it was defeated by national resistance and a peaceful government change was achieved.

Since that, in South Korea, South Korean people have been making progress in political democratization and political democracy.

South Korea suffered a foreign exchange crisis which was managed by the IMF. However, South Korea has been achieving relatively stable economic growth. Although South Korea has been in a delicate geopolitical position among neighboring superpower countries, it was involved in hosting the Summer Olympics in 1988 and joining the OECD and G20 in the 1990s. Meanwhile, South Korea has been increasing its international recognition and importance. Also, South Korea has established a state of peace through cooperation with North Korean and the inter-Korean summits.

III. Political System

10. The Constitution of South Korea was enacted and enforced in July 1948, and it has been revised nine times in the process of political upheaval in the 1960s and 1970s. Even after that, in the presidential elections, constitutional amendments, including the forms of government and the presidential term, have been discussed. However, considering the unfavorable experience of arbitrary constitutional amendments by force, the South Constitution has remained unchanged since the full revision in 1987.

According to Article 130 of the South Korean Constitution, a resolution of the National Assembly must be obtained by the approval of two-thirds or more of the total number of members of the National Assembly. After the resolution of the National Assembly has been obtained, the National Assembly shall decide upon the proposed amendments within sixty days of the public announcement, and passage by the National Assembly shall require the concurrent vote of two-thirds or more of the total members of the National Assembly.

11. The Constitution, which is the supreme norm in Korea's national law and order system, consists of (1) the principles of popular sovereignty and democracy, (2) the principle of legislative parliamentaryism, the rule of law, and (3) the separation of powers.

First, regarding the principles of popular sovereignty and democracy, Article 1 (1) of the South Korean Constitution proclaims that the Republic of Korea shall be a democratic republic and (2) provides that the sovereignty of the Republic of Korea shall reside in the people, and all state authority shall emanate from the people.

In paragraph 2, "The sovereignty of the Republic of Korea rests with the people, and all powers belong to the people." In this way, the Constitution provides freedom for the people to make decisions about the state. Thus, it is guaranteed as the highest standard of the country that South Korean people can participate in its decision-making.

Second, concerning the principle of legislative parliamentaryism and the rule of law, Article 40 of the South Korean Constitution provides that the legislative power shall be vested in the National Assembly. By adopting representative parliamentaryism as a political expression, the Constitution is a practical limit to the exercise of sovereignty by the people. In addition, the matters concerning the rights and obligations of citizens must be determined by law and their contents must conform to the fundamental ideology of the Constitution. It is "the rule of law." This principle is also recognized as a basic principle of the Constitution.

Third, the Constitution adopts the principle of separation of powers that seeks to maintain mutual checks and balances by dividing into the legislative, administrative, and judicial systems. The relationship between the legislative power and the executive power in the separation of rights during the political turmoil of the 1960s and 1970s and after that was still unresolved.

There were times when the elements of the parliamentary system were strong in South Korea, but the elements of the strong presidential system have generally been South Korean government forms.

12. The South Korean Constitution provides, "All citizens shall be assured of human worth and dignity and have the right to pursuit of happiness. It shall be the duty of the State to confirm and guarantee the fundamental and inviolable human rights of individuals." (Article 10 of the South Korean Constitution). Also, Article 37(1) of the South Korean Constitution says that freedom and rights of citizens shall not be neglected on the grounds that they are not enumerated in the Constitution.

According to Article 10 of the Korean Constitution, the realization of "human dignity and value" and the guarantee of the right to pursue happiness are fundamental. And Article 11(1) of the South Korean Constitution provides that all citizens shall be equal before the law, and there shall be no discrimination in political, economic, social, or cultural life on account of sex, religion, or social status.

Thus, it guarantees equal rights. And although the Korean constitution was revised due to the change of government, the rights to personal, mental, privacy and social and economic security and freedom have been widely guaranteed. Substantial and procedural guarantees regarding bodily freedom (such as freedom of the body and the principle of the criminal justice system), freedom of conscience, freedom of religion, freedom of academic and artistic freedom, freedom of speech & publication, and freedom of assembly & association are guaranteed. In addition, the South Korean Constitution guarantees freedom of residence and movement, freedom of occupation, and property rights as social and economic freedom. Also, the right to receive education, free compulsory education, the right to work and the right to organize labor unions are stipulated as the basic rights in the Constitution.

13. According to the South Korean Constitution, the president is the head of state and the head of government at the same time. The president is elected by direct popular vote. The term of office of the President is five years, and the President shall not be reelected. (Article 70). According to the Korean constitution, the president can exercise powers in all areas of state affairs.

(1) As the president's authority on the constitution of constitutional institutions, the president has the authority to organize administrative organs by exercising the power to appoint the prime minister, members of the State Council, heads of various administrative departments, and important public officials as the head of the

executive power. The President has the authority to organize constitutional institutions other than the executive branch (especially the right to appoint the Chief Justice of the Supreme Court and Supreme Court Justices and the right to appoint the Chief Justice of the Constitutional Court and Constitutional Court Judges). (2) As the president's authority to legislate, (a) the president may propose a constitutional amendment, and (b) the president submits a bill to the National Assembly after deliberation by the State Council or raises an objection when there is an objection to a bill passed by the National Assembly. The President can then ask the Parliament for reconsideration. Also, (c) The President may issue presidential decrees concerning matters delegated to him/her by Act with the scope specifically defined and also matters necessary to enforce Acts. Furthermore, the president may request the assembly of an extraordinary session of the National Assembly.

(3) The powers of the President with respect to judicial affairs include: (a) the right to form the Supreme Court and the Constitutional Court; (b) the right to sue for dissolution of a political party whose purpose or activity is contrary to the basic democratic order; and (c) as prescribed by law, amnesty, commutation or re-instatement may be ordered.

In addition, (4) the president, who is the head of administrative powers, (a) has the highest authority to make and execute policies regarding administration, (b) has the right to command the Armed Forces, and (c) has the right to appoint and dismiss public officials. In addition, (5) the President has the right to refer to the referendum to apply important policies related to foreign affairs, national defense, unification, and other important national security policies to the referendum if deemed necessary. The President can exercise national emergency rights, such as emergency orders and emergency financial and economic actions or orders, and the President has right to declaration and termination of martial law.

14. The National Assembly forms the central axis of parliamentaryism, one of the basic principles of the Korean Constitution. The National Assembly, the representative body of the people, adopts a unicameral system and consists of members of the National Assembly elected by the people's universal, equal, direct, and secret elections. Members of the National Assembly can be reappointed for a four-year term, and they are divided into the local constituency members, who are elected according to the relative majority representation system and the national members of the national constituency, which are distributed in proportion to the votes of each political party.

As the powers of the National Assembly, it (1) has legislative power with respect to the basic function of the legislative action, (2) has national finances through deliberation and confirmation of the budget, and (3) plays the role of a state control body. The National Assembly's main powers to control state affairs include: (1) the right to consent to the appointment of the president as the prime minister in relations with the government, the right to inspect and investigate state affairs, the right to consent to the appointment and hearing of major public officials, the right to vote on impeachment charges against the president, and the right to vote on impeachment proceedings against the President; (2) the right to consent to the appointment of the Chief Justice of the Supreme Court, the Supreme Court, and the President of the Constitutional Court, the right to elect three judges of the Constitutional Court, and the right to enact laws for the establishment and organization of the courts and the Constitutional Court.

The South Korean constitution freely recognizes the establishment of political parties, which are the cornerstones of parliamentary democracy, and guarantees multiple parties. In Korea since 1945, in a broad sense, parties representing the conservative and democratic forces have been compatible. However, since the collapse of the dictatorship in the late 1980s and the rise of a civilian government in the country, it has been divided since the recent impeachment of former President Park Geun-hye. Due to the further division of the conservative forces, as of April 2023, two major parties held most of the seats in the National Assembly. If the Democratic and Peace Party, as the first party, can be said to be the historical successor group of the democratic forces that opposed the dictatorship in the past, the Liberty Korea Party is considered to represent the conservative force as the second party.

15. Judicial power belongs to the courts according to the South Korean Constitution. In addition to having jurisdiction over legal disputes, the courts have the right to request an adjudication on the constitutionality of the law. The Supreme Court has the power to make a final review of the constitutionality or legality of administrative decrees, regulations or actions, when their constitutionality or legality is at issue in a trial.

According to the Constitution of Korea, although the Supreme Court is recognized as the highest court, the Constitutional Court has a separate constitution. It has the power to adjudicate impeachment and to adjudicate the dissolution of an unconstitutional political party. The Constitutional Court, one of the highest judicial organs along with the Supreme Court, is composed of nine judges with the qualifications of judges, and the judges are appointed by the president. Among the judges, three are elected by the National Assembly, and three are appointed by the Chief Justice of the Supreme Court. The President of the Constitutional Court is appointed by the President from among the judges with the consent of the National Assembly. Constitutional judges serve a six-year term and may be reappointed.

16. Although Korea has a centralized state of a single state, it has adopted the local autonomy system as a complement. According to Article 117 of the Constitution, local governments deal with administrative matters pertaining to the welfare of local residents, manage properties, and enact provisions relating to local autonomy, within the limit of Acts and subordinate statutes. And the types of local governments are determined by the Act. The organs of local governments include the local council, which is the decision-making body, and the head of the local government, which is the executive body.

IV. Economy and Society

17. Since 1945, when Korea was liberated from Japan, it has experienced rapid economic growth, moving from an underdeveloped country to a developed country through a developing country. According to the IMF, in 2020, South Korea was ranked 10th in the world with a GDP of USD 1.6 trillion and GDP per capita of USD 31,638. In response to the lack of resources and capital and the need for rapid industrialization, South Korea proceeded with strong state-led economic development during the industrialization process of the 1960s and 1970s and established a corporate economic structure centered on large corporations with chaebol rather than SMEs as the mainstay. It has been promoting export-led economic growth with processing trade as its core. Major trading partners include the United States, China, Japan, Taiwan, Germany, United Kingdom, Indonesia and Malaysia. South Korea's manufacturing industry tends to be concentrated in industries that require intermediate-level skills, and major industries include shipbuilding, electronics, automobiles, and semiconductors.

18. The economic order of South Korea is based on respect for the freedom and creative initiative of enterprises and individuals in economic affairs. The State may regulate and coordinate economic affairs to maintain the balanced growth and stability of the national economy, to ensure proper distribution of income, to prevent the domination of the market and the abuse of economic power and to democratize the economy through harmony among the economic agents. (Article 119 of the Constitution). Therefore, South Korea's economic order is evaluated as a social market economy order according to the Constitution. It is a form of promoting democratization of the economy through state coordination and regulation based on the market economy order and the order of guaranteeing property rights. In order to realize the principle of social market economic order, the South Korean Constitution includes: (1) the principle of private enterprise and determination by law on the national and public ownership of enterprises, (2) the principle of economic freedom, (3) the protection and nurturing of farmers, fishermen and SMEs, (4) guarantee of the consumer protection movement, and (5) the promotion and freedom of foreign trade and innovation in science and technology.

19. South Korea started to introduce a modern social welfare system in the 1960s and 1970s as social problems such as industrial accidents and rich-poor conflicts caused by rapid economic growth intensified. Industrial accident compensation insurance, medical insurance, and military pension were introduced in the early 1960s, but in the 1980s and 1990s, nationwide medical insurance was implemented and an insurance system for industrial accidents and job insecurity was established. In addition, the South Korean government has been expanding various social security systems to ensure a minimum standard of living for the poor and to improve the welfare of the elderly, the disabled and children.

20. After liberation in 1945, Korea was divided into North and South along the 38th parallel. Even after the armistice, South Korea and North Korea have experienced serious confrontations, including local armed conflict. Then, at the global level, with the end of the Cold War, the fall of the military regime in South Korea, and the emergence of a civilian government, humanitarian exchanges such as the reunion of separated families between the two Koreas began in 1985. The state of peace is gradually being established, with inter-Korean summits being held in North

Korea. The Korean Constitution declares in its preamble that the peaceful unification of the South and the North is the historical mission of the Republic of Korea.

§2. Legal System

I. The Supremacy of the Legislature and the Law

21. The South Korean Constitution adopts the principle of separation of powers as one of its basic principles and separates the powers of legislation, administration and justice from the point of view of mutual checks and balances. South Korea's legal system belongs to the continental legal system based on the supremacy of legislative power under the influence of European, especially German, and French legal systems through Japan. Therefore, the executive and judiciary must also be bound by the constitution and laws enacted by the legislative branch. On the other hand, there is a hierarchical order between legal norms, so the laws must not violate the higher-order constitution, and the fundamental idea of the constitution must be considered in the interpretation and application of legal regulations. For example, Article 750 of the Korean Civil Code[2] stipulates liability for damages resulting from unlawful acts. In determining which acts are unlawful, the provisions on guaranteeing basic rights of the Constitution serve as an important interpretation.

22. The executive and judiciary must be bound by the Constitution and laws and have legitimate powers only to the extent permitted by law in making administrative orders or judicial rules themselves. The codified general law will function as a living norm for an individual's legal relationship by applying it to specific cases in the process of performance of duties by public officials or judges. In some cases, the interpretation of laws is prescribed by individual laws, but in general, the following methods of interpretation are accepted: (1) literal interpretation to reveal the literal meaning of legal norms, (2) considering systematically with other provisions of the law, a systematic interpretation that seeks to understand the meaning under the relevant circumstances, (3) a historical interpretation that seeks to reveal the meaning of a regulation according to the will of the legislator, and (4) a purposeful interpretation that seeks to interpret the meaning of a legal norm in accordance with the normative purpose of the law. In South Korea, the comparative methods that compare and consider relevant legal principles of Japan, Germany, France and the United States have frequently been used in the interpretation and application of such laws.

23. Even if legislators try to enact perfect norms, there are cases where the enacted laws are incomplete and have flaws in the discipline of related legal relations. Even in this case, the judge cannot refuse the trial, so she can apply analogy, that is, extend and apply one legal provision to other cases in light of the purpose of the norm. To this extent, judges play the role of enacting laws themselves when

2. Korea Legislation Research Institute translates its title as "Civil Act." However, these authors understand "Civil Code" would be appropriate in comparative law perspective.

there are flaws in the law. Furthermore, if there is no law, judges must follow practices and nature of things, and precedents are also effectively functioning as courts. The judgment of the court only has binding force as a standard only in the case concerned and does not have the general binding force like the law. Therefore, although court decisions cannot become a source of law in Korea, precedents are effectively binding as "living laws" in that lower courts do not easily deviate from the judgments of the Supreme Court, which is the highest court, in similar cases. In the case of tort liability under Article 750 of the Korean Civil code, which is in the form of a general provision, a series of case law plays an important role in Korea as well.

II. The Role of the Judiciary

24. According to Article 101(1) of the Constitution, the judicial power belongs to the court, which is made up of judges. The courts are composed of the Supreme Court, which is the highest court, and the lower courts. The lower courts are divided into six types: the High Court, the Patent Court, the District Court, the Family Court, the Administrative Court, and the Rehabilitation Court. The Patent Court and the Rehabilitation Court are high court-level courts in charge of patent and rehabilitation cases, respectively. Therefore, the basic structure of the court organization has a hierarchical structure of the Supreme Court, the High Court, and the District Court. The Constitutional Court is in charge of constitutional adjudication, such as adjudication of unconstitutional laws and adjudication of constitutional complaints to ensure basic rights. Special courts are prohibited in principle, but military courts may be established as special courts to have jurisdiction over military trials. As a judicial body in South Korea, the courts are made up of only professional judges[3] and do not adopt the jury system recognized in the United States and the United States.

25. Courts in charge of general civil and criminal cases include the Supreme Court, High Court, and District Court, and the District Court is the Court of First Instance. The district court may have branch offices and city courts, county courts within the jurisdiction of the district court to handle part of the affairs.[4] However, important cases, such as death penalty, life imprisonment or imprisonment without prison labor for a short period of one year or longer, and civil cases in which the value of the litigation exceeds KRW 200 million, are judged by a collegiate panel consisting of three judges. The municipal court or county court, which is an affiliated organization of the district court, has a small civil case that can be dealt with quickly according to a simple procedure (in its simple procedure, payment of a certain amount of money or other substitutes or securities whose value for the purpose of litigation does not exceed KRW 30 million). It has jurisdiction over civil cases of

3. However, in the case of a case requiring specialized knowledge, an expert in the relevant field may participate as a professional examiner in the litigation procedure at the request of the party or ex officio in order to supplement the expertise of the trial.
4. Subdivision, city and county courts are provided for the convenience of residents who live far from the main office of the district court and are not separate courts from the district court (The Court Organization Act, Art. 3, para. 2).

the first trial for the purpose of the superior court of the district court, is a high court, and has jurisdiction over cases of appeal or appeal against the judgment, decision, and order of the first instance of the collegiate panel of the district court.[5] High Courts are located in five locations in South Korea and exercise their jurisdiction in a collegiate panel composed of three judges. The Supreme Court of South Korea is the Supreme Court and is located in Seoul. The Supreme Court is made up of thirteen Supreme Court Justices and has a full body composed of more than two-thirds of all Supreme Court Justices and a Department consisting of three or more Supreme Court Justices. The appeals trial, which is overseen by the Supreme Court, is subject to the final judgment rendered by the high court or the district court collegiate (appellate division) as the second instance and has the character of a legal trial.

III. Distinguishing Between Public Law and Private Law

26. In South Korea, there is a strict distinction between public law and private law. While the latter is the law governing the private rights, obligations and legal relations between Korean citizens and foreigners residing in South Korea, the former is all of laws and regulations governing the public activities of the state or local government exercising national sovereignty. Depending on the distinction between public and private law, the applicable laws regarding the relevant legal relationship and the competent court will be different. Private law relations are governed by the Korean Civil Code or individual special civil laws and if they fall under the jurisdiction of the ordinary court. However, public law relations are legal relations under public law, and the administrative courts have jurisdiction.

27. Various views are suggested in theories regarding the standard for distinguishing between public law and private law. Depending on whether the legal relationship is an unequal relationship of power and obedience or a relationship of equality and equality, in the former case, it is public law, but in the latter case, it is understood as private law. Therefore, according to the South Korean courts, even in the case of a public contract in which a local government is a contracting party, the local government belongs to a private contract concluded on an equal footing with the other party as the subject of the private economy. It is said that there is no difference, and unless otherwise specified, legal principles such as private autonomy and freedom of contract apply.[6] In addition, administrative litigation has characteristics that are distinct from civil litigation. If the procedure of civil litigation is dominated by an adversary system and *dispositionalism* according to the principle of private freedom, administrative litigation has features of arbitrary administrative adjudication *prepositionalism* and examining the case ex officio according to the characteristics of administrative cases.

---

5. However, cases of appeal or appeal against the judgment, decision, or order of a single judge of the district court are under the jurisdiction of the collegiate panel of the district court main body (The Court Organization Act, Art. 32 para. 2).
6. Supreme Court Decision 2019Ma267464 Decided Dec. 13, 2019.

IV. General Source of Private Law and Courts of Tort Law

28. The source of law is the current or existing form of legal norms that judges must comply with in their judgment. The source of law is divided into written law and unwritten law. The Constitution is the highest standard in the national legal and order system and serves as the basis for various sub-norms and interpretations. It guarantees the inviolable basic rights of individuals. Accordingly, the effect of the source of law is invalid if the lower-level laws or customary laws are against the value order of the Constitution. In addition, the basic rights guaranteed by the Constitution influence the legal relationship between individuals in addition to the public legal relationship through the general provisions of private law. The most important written private law in the judicial system is a law in a formal sense, that is, a law passed by the National Assembly and promulgated by the president. In the case of civil affairs, the Korean Civil Code is the most important law, and there are various special civil laws (such as the Housing Lease Protection Act) enacted to supplement or amend the Civil Code. In the written law, there are: (1) executive orders issued by state agencies (president, prime minister, administrative departments) other than the National Assembly through a certain procedure, (2) Supreme Court Rules established by the Supreme Court regarding litigation procedures, court affairs, etc., to the extent that it does not conflict with the law, and (3) autonomous laws and regulations enacted by local governments regarding their affairs within the scope of laws and regulations (ordinances enacted by local councils, rules enacted by the heads of local governments). Treaties concluded and promulgated by the Constitution and generally recognized international laws also become sources of law. However, there is customary law as unwritten law. Customary law refers to a norm by which a practice that has arisen on its own in social life has reached the point of obtaining legal certainty. Article 1 of the Korean Civil Code and Commercial Code explicitly recognizes that the customary law is the applicable law. Regarding precedents, which are norms formed through court trials, the majority position does not recognize as the source of law (*see* 23 above).

29. The Korean Civil Code was promulgated in 1958 after the Korean War and after the establishment of the government in 1948, and it was put into effect in 1960. The Korean Civil Code was basically enacted based on the Japanese civil law at that time, and in the process, the Civil Codes of Germany, France, Switzerland and other countries were referenced and reflected. According to the German Pandecten system, the Korean Civil Code consists of five parts: general provisions, real rights, claims, relatives and inheritance. Since its enactment, the Korean Civil Code has undergone a total of thirty-three revisions as of January 2021, mainly in terms of relatives and inheritance.

30. South Korea's tort laws are mainly stipulated in Articles 750 through 766 of the Korean Civil Code. In addition to the Civil Code, individual laws function as sources of law of tort, such as the National Compensation Act, the Product Liability Act, the Automobile Damage Guarantee Act, the Nuclear Damage Compensation Act, and the Act on Liability and Relief for Environmental Pollution Damage. The provisions of damages are mainly stipulated in Articles 393 through 399 of the

Korean Civil Code. These provisions, which are applied to compensation for damages caused by breach of contract, are applied *mutatis mutandis* to tort liability according to Article 763 of the Korean Civil Code.

31. Delict acts in the Civil Code are divided into general delict acts under Article 750 and special delict acts under Articles 755 through 760 in the establishment of responsibility. Among them, the general tort of Article 750 mainly consists of: (1) unlawful offense and (2) intentional or negligent offense. Due to this, there is a risk of harming legal stability by ambiguity about what kind of act is delict act, but it provides room for the court to apply it flexibly according to the changing social situation according to the case law. The main provisions of the Korean Civil Code regarding torts and damages are as follows.

Article 750 (Definition of Torts):

> Any person who causes losses to or inflicts injuries on another person by an unlawful act, intentionally or negligently, shall be bound to make compensation for damages arising therefrom.

Article 751 (Compensation for Non-Economic Damages):

(1) A person who has injured the person, liberty or fame of another or has inflicted any mental anguish to another person shall be liable to make compensation for damages arising therefrom.
(2) The court may order the guilty party to discharge the compensation mentioned in paragraph (1) by periodical payments, and may order such guilty parties to offer reasonable security in order to insure his performance of such obligations.

Article 752 (Consolation Money where of Violation of Life):

> A person who has caused the death of another person shall be liable for damages to the lineal ascendants, lineal descendants and the spouse, even where no economic damages exist as a result thereof.

Article 753 (Minor's Competency):

> In the event that a minor has caused damage to another, if he was not in possession of sufficient intelligence to understand his responsibility for the act, he shall not be liable for damages resulting therefrom.

Article 754 (Competency of Person of Mental Unsoundness):

> A person who, while in a state of mental unsoundness, has caused damage to another, shall not be liable for damages resulting therefrom: Provided, That this shall not be the case, if he has brought upon himself his state of mental unsoundness either intentionally or negligently.

Article 755 (Supervisor's Liability):

(1) If a person who has caused any damage to another is exempt from liabilities under Article 753 or 754, the person who is under a legal duty to supervise such person shall be liable to make compensation for the damage: Provided, That the same shall not apply, if the person so supervising has not been negligent in performing his/her duty of supervision.
(2) A person who supervises a person who has no liability in accordance with Article 753 or 754 on behalf of a person whose duty is to supervise shall also assume the same liability as set forth in paragraph (1).

Article 756 (Employer's Liability for Compensation):

(1) A person who employs another to perform a specific affair is liable for compensating for any loss inflicted on a third person by the employee in the course of performing the specific affair: Provided, That this shall not apply where the employer has exercised due care in appointing the employee, and in supervising the performance of the specific affair, or where the loss has been inflicted even if the employer has exercised due care.
(2) A person who supervises the performance of a specific affair on behalf of the employer shall also assume the same liability as prescribed in paragraph (1).
(3) In cases falling under paragraphs (1) and (2), the employer or the supervisor may claim for reimbursement from the employee.

Article 757 (Liability of Person who Ordered Work to be Done):

The person who placed an order for a work to be done shall not be bound to make compensation for any damages caused to a third person by the contractor with respect to such work: Provided, That this shall not be the case, if the former was guilty of gross negligence in placing the order, or in providing instructions therefor.

Article 758 (Liability of Possessor, Owner of Structure, etc.):

(1) If any damages has been caused to another person by reason of any defect in the construction or maintenance of a structure, the person in possession of the structure shall be liable for such damages: Provided, That if the person in possession has exercised due care in order to prevent the occurrence of such damages, compensation for the damage shall be made by the owner.
(2) The provisions of paragraph (1) shall apply mutatis mutandis where there exists any defect in the planting or maintenance of trees.
(3) In cases of paragraphs (1) and (2), the possessor or the owner may exercise the right to obtain reimbursement from the person to whom the damages are attributable.

Article 759 (Liability of Possessor of Animals):

(1) Every possessor of an animal is liable for any loss inflicted on a third person by the animal: Provided, That this shall not apply where the possessor has not been negligent in giving due care in taking custody of the animal according to the species and nature of the animal.
(2) Any person who takes custody of an animal on behalf of the possessor of the animal shall also assume the same liability as prescribed in paragraph (1).

Article 760 (Liability of Joint Tort-feasors):

(1) If two or more persons have by their joint unlawful acts caused damages to another, they shall be jointly and severally liable to make compensation for such damages.
(2) The provisions of paragraph (1) shall also apply if it is impossible to ascertain which of the participants, albeit not joint, has caused the damages.
(3) Instigators and accessories shall be deemed to act jointly.

Article 761 (Self-Defense and Act of Necessity):

(1) A person who, in order to protect his own interest or that of a third person against an unlawful act of another, unavoidably causes damages to another person shall not be liable for such damages: Provided, That the injured party may claim for damages in respect of the unlawful act.
(2) The provisions of paragraph (1) shall apply mutatis mutandis where a person unavoidably caused damages to another person in order to avert an imminent danger.

Article 762 (Status of Unborn Child in respect of Claims for Damage):

An embryo or fetus shall, in respect of the claim for damages, be deemed to have been already born.

Article 763 (Applicable Provisions to be Applied Mutatis Mutandis):

The provisions of Articles 393, 394, 396 and 399 shall apply mutatis mutandis to torts claims.

Article 764 (Special Rules Applicable to Defamation):

The court may, on the application of the injured party, order the person who has defamed another's reputation to take measures appropriate for repairing the injured party's reputation, either in lieu of, or together with provision of compensation.

Article 765 (Application for Reduction in Compensation Amount):

(1) The person liable to make compensation in accordance with the provisions of this Chapter may petition the court for a reduction in the amount of

compensation, if the damages were caused neither intentionally nor by gross negligence, and such payments of compensation shall be a severe hardship to his livelihood.

(2) The court may, if the petition mentioned in paragraph (1) has been filed, reduce the amount of compensation after a study of the claimant's and obligor's respective financial situations and the cause giving rise to the damages.

Article 766 (Prescription in respect of Right to Claim for Damages):

(1) The right to claim for damages resulting from an unlawful act shall lapse by prescription if not exercised within three years commencing from the date on which the injured party or his/her legal representative becomes aware of such damage and of the identity of the person who caused it.
(2) The provisions of paragraph (1) shall also apply if ten years have elapsed from the time when the unlawful act was committed.
(3) Where a minor suffers from sexual violence, sexual molestation, sexual harassment, other sexual infringement, the extinctive prescription of the right to claim compensation for damages shall not proceed until such minor attain the majority.

Article 393 (Scope of Compensation for Damages):

(1) The compensation for damages arising from the non-performance of an obligation shall be limited to ordinary damages.
(2) The obligor is responsible for reparation for damages that have arisen through special circumstances, only if he had foreseen or could have foreseen such circumstances.

Article 394 (Method of Compensation for Damages):

Unless otherwise agreed by the parties, the damages shall be recovered in money.

Article 396 (Comparative Negligence):[7]

If there has been any negligence on the part of the obligee in regard to the non-performance of the obligation, the court shall take it into account in determining the liability for and assessing the amount of the damages.

Article 399 (Obligor's Subrogation to Obligee owing to Compensation for Damages):

7. The title is "contributory negligence." But these authors translate it comparative negligence to deliver its proper meaning.

If an obligee has received by way of damages the full value of the thing or right which forms the subject of the claim, the obligor shall ipso jure be subrogated to the position of the obligee in respect of such thing or right.

§3. Function of Tort Law

32. Liability for torts consists of: (1) the function of compensating for damage caused to the victim due to the tortious act (compensation function) and (2) the function of preventing and deterring potential offenders from harming the victim by having the tortfeasor compensate the victim for the damage (preventive function). The dominant view in South Korea is that it does not recognize the function (sanctioning function) of civil tortious liability to sanction tortfeasors.[8]

33. Regarding the relationship between the compensation function and the preventive function, the dominant view in South Korea is that the primary purpose of civil tort liability is to compensate the victim for damages. Therefore, civil liability is meant to restore the victim to a state that would have existed if there had been no harm done. In addition, as far as tort liability is recognized, civil liability for damages is for the purpose of compensating for damages resulting from the difference between the victim's property status due to the tortious act and the state of assumptive property that would have been in the absence of the tortious act, as far as tort liability is recognized. In principle, there is no distinction between the degree of intention and negligence of the tortfeasor in determining the scope of damages, unlike English and American tort law. Therefore, even if tort liability aims to deter potential tortfeasors from committing illegal acts through damages, it is evaluated as a byproduct of its compensation function.

34. As explained in 33, the prevailing view is that the main function of the damage compensation law is to be found in the compensation for damages. However, recently, the function of deterring and preventing illegal acts through civil damages has been emphasized and legislated.

In order to eradicate the practice of subcontracting, in the case of certain unfair trading practices, Article 35(2) of the Fair Transactions in Subcontracting Act provides that the prime contractor shall be liable to compensate the injury or loss to the extent not exceeding three times the injury or loss inflicted upon the person. This liability for compensation (the treble damages) is further extended to prevent discriminatory acts between fixed-term workers and part-time workers. Such liability for damages is recognized not only in the act of leakage of personal information by business operators but also in the Product Liability Act of 2018. Article 3(2) of the Product Liability Act provides that a manufacturer shall compensate for damages to the life, body or property of a person caused by a defect of a product. Thus, if a manufacturer causes serious damage to life or body of a person as a result of not

8. *See* Park, Dong Jin, *The Commentary of Korean Civil Code—Law of Obligations (6)*, 23–36, 2022.

taking necessary measures against a defect of a product despite the manufacturer's knowledge of such defect, the manufacturer shall be liable up to three times the damage sustained by the person.

However, with respect to non-economic damages, the deterrent function of tort liability has been emphasized in the traditional view. Moreover, in 2017, the court prepared and announced the guidelines for calculating non-economic damages for each type of tortious acts: (1) traffic accident, (2) mass casualty accident, (3) commercial tortious act, and (4) defamation. In these cases, the role of liability for damages for deterrence and prevention of tortious acts is clearly defined by determining that the amount of compensation can be increased according to the circumstances of the offense, the intention of the tortfeasor, and the degree of reproachability.

§4. Relationship Between Tort and Criminal Law

35. In South Korea, there is a strict distinction between tortious acts and criminal law. The Korean criminal law is codified in the Korean Criminal Code,[9] which was enacted in 1953, earlier than the Korean Civil Code. Whereas the Korean Civil Code provides for the general elements of tort in Article 750, the Korean Criminal Code separately lists the acts that constitute a crime, including felonies such as murder and assault and misdemeanors such as criminal mischief. The Korean Criminal Procedure Act stipulates the procedure for criminal litigation. Criminal litigation differs from civil litigation, which is a procedure for resolving disputes between individual rights and legal relations, while criminal litigation deals with cases related to the exercise of the state's criminal right to private persons.

36. There is a fundamental difference between tort and criminal law in purpose and function. The former is a private law system that aims to compensate the victim for the purpose of protecting the legal interests of the victim. The latter is a public law system, which aims to prevent the occurrence of harm or retaliation against criminals by understanding crime as a harm to the state and society. Therefore, whether to claim damages for civil liability is determined by the individual decision-making of the victim. However, in criminal proceedings, the protection of the legal interests of the state and society rather than the personal interests of the victim is prioritized, and therefore, the public prosecutor, a state institution, has the right to prosecute.

In addition, since civil and criminal liability have different purposes and functions, the requirements for liability are different. For example, in the case of the Criminal Law, the principle is punishment for intentional criminals. However, in civil liability, compensation for damages is recognized without distinction in intention or negligence. Therefore, a tortious act giving rise to civil liability does not always constitute a criminal offense.

9. Korea Legislation Research Institute translates its title as "Criminal Act." However, these authors understand "Criminal Code" would be proper in comparative law perspective.

37. Although civil liability and criminal liability have different purposes and functions, there are cases in which a single offense constitutes both liability, such as murder or fraud. Even in this case, civil and criminal litigation have different purposes and evaluation values, and each litigation procedure has an independent nature. Therefore, the results of both trials may be different because the same evidence has different values in both cases.

Nevertheless, both lawsuits influence each other, and civil judgments that have a general effect, such as formative judgments, binding criminal judgments, and facts recognized in related criminal judgments, can be powerful evidence in civil lawsuits. In addition, it is against the economy of litigation that both civil and criminal lawsuits are conducted for a single case, and there is a risk of inconsistency in the trial by judging the same evidence differently in both lawsuits. Thus, when a conviction is to be declared in the procedures of a criminal trial, the court may request the order compensation for direct physical damage, medical expenses, and solatium that has occurred due to the criminal acts of the accused case. (Article 25 of the Act on Special Cases Concerning Expedition of Legal Proceedings).

§5. Relationship Between Contract and Tort Liability

38. The Korean Civil Code distinguishes between contract liability and tort liability. The former deals with cases where the other parties are damaged by violating the obligations stipulated in the contractual relationship. The latter deals with cases where there are tortious acts but no special relationship between the tortfeasors and the victims. Both contract liability and tort liability are negligent in principle (Articles 390[10] and 750 of the Korean Civil Code), but there are some important differences as follows. First, with respect to the burden of proof of intention or negligence, in the case of tort liability, the victim claiming damages must prove the intentional or negligence of the perpetrator, whereas, in the case of contract liability, the debtor has proven that there was no intentional or negligent negligence to have no contractual liability. In addition, in the case of tort liability, a person who employs another to perform a specific affair is liable for compensating for any loss inflicted on a third person by the employee in the course of performing the specific affair. However, it does not apply where the employer has exercised due care in appointing the employee and supervising the performance of the specific affair (Article 756(1) of the Korean Civil Code). However, in the case of contract liability, where a legal representative for the obligor affects performance in lieu of the latter or the obligor affects performance through the other person as an employee, the intention or negligence of the legal representative or the other person shall be deemed as that of the obligor (Article 391 of the Korean Civil Code).

10. Article 390 (Non-performance of Obligations and Compensation for Damages):

> If an obligor fails to effect performance in accordance with the tenor and purport of the obligation, the obligee may claim damages: Provided, That this shall not apply to where performance has become impossible and where this is not due to the obligor's intention or negligence.

Furthermore, with respect to the extinctive prescription, the right to claim for damages resulting from an unlawful act lapses by prescription: (1) within three years commencing from the date on which the injured party becomes aware of such damage and of the identity of the tortfeasor, or (2) if ten years had elapsed from the time when the unlawful act was committed (Article 766 of the Korean Civil Code).[11] However, the right to claim compensation for damages pursuant to contract liability has a prescription of ten years, unless otherwise specified (Article 162(1) of the Korean Civil Code).

39. The contract liability comes from a liability relationship between the contracting parties. But tort liability comes from cases where there is no contractual relationship between a tortfeasor and a victim. Thus, when a breach of a contract constitutes a tortious act, tort liability as well as contract liability would be an issue. For example, if a taxi driver causes bodily harm to a passenger due to negligence in operation or if the lessee damages the object of the rent contract, both the breach of contract and liability for tort may be problematic at the same time. Although the Korean Civil Law scholars' opinions have been in dispute, many scholars and precedents have supported the view that the victim can ask for damages based on contract or tort liability, according to his/her choice. In other words, it takes the principle of contention of claims. Therefore, both claims are established independently of each other and do not exclude each other, and even if a special agreement of immunity for breach of contract is made, it is not naturally applied to tort liability unless there is an explicit or implied agreement to apply it to tort liability.[12]

40. In view of the difference between contract liability and tort liability, especially in relation to the burden of proof of intention or negligence and the responsibility for subrogation for the acts of others, the South Korean doctrine is based on the circumstance that the contractual liability is more advantageous to the claimant, the victim, than the tortious liability. In the case of a special relationship similar to a contract, especially in the case of illegally infringing the life, body, or pure property interests of the negotiating party in the course of contract negotiation, the contractual negligence in concluding the contract to extend contract liability rather than tort liability (pre-contractual liability theory (*culpa in contrahendo*)) has been being argued.[13] However, South Korean precedents are unaware of the need to extend contract liability to non-contractual relationships as the victim's burden of proof has been relaxed and the employer's proof of immunity has not been actually recognized in subrogation responsibility. In fact, South Korean precedent applies tort liability in the case of unfair breach of contract negotiations.

In addition, in some countries, the principle of contract has protective effects for a third party against pure property damage caused by loss of investment by a third

11. Article 766(3) was added on Oct. 20, 2020. It provides that where a minor suffers from sexual violence, sexual molestation, sexual harassment, other sexual infringement, the extinctive prescription of the right to claim compensation for damages shall not proceed until such minor attain the majority.
12. Supreme Court Decision 2005Da3724 Decided Oct. 13, 2006.
13. SONG, Tuck-Soo, *Law of Obligations—Special Parts*, 6th ed., 65–66, Parkyoungsa, 2023.

party due to misinformation of professional experts such as certified public accountants. They have developed and applied contractual liabilities. However, South Korean precedents have acknowledged the tort liability of the wrong information provider by utilizing the openness of the liability component under Article 750 of the Korean Civil Code.[14]

41. Regarding the scope of contract liability and tort liability or the effect of contract law on tort liability, the Korean Supreme Court recently made an interesting decision on a case in the comparative law aspect. In this case, the Supreme Court made its *en banc* decision, in which a person who had caused soil pollution on his own land illegally buried waste and sold it to a buyer. Later, the land was sold to other buyers several times. The issue of the case was whether the first seller of the land was obliged to damages equivalent to the cost of cleaning up contaminated soil or disposing of waste to the final buyer.[15] In this regard, four of the thirteen Justices made their minority view that in the case where waste was buried in his land, or the soil was polluted and distributed, the seller shall not bear tort liability for damage in waste treatment costs or pollution remediation costs in relation to the final buyer of the land that has no direct transaction relationship with him. The minority view was based on: (1) the principle of the buyer's risk bearing and (2) the distribution of disadvantages due to defects or harms to the object of sale within the contracting parties who buried waste in their land or polluted the soil in accordance with the principle of the buyer's risk for the condition of the object of sale and the distribution of disadvantages due to defects or harm to the object of sale within the contracting parties.

However, the majority opinion said, "Even if the owner of the land causes soil pollution, if he sold it by providing the land containing the contaminated soil, it constitutes a tortious act against his buyer and buyers of the land later." Although the majority opinion is inconsistent with the idea of predominance of contract law that contract-related incidents are sufficient to be resolved by contract law, their supplementary opinion stated the following: (1) the degree of illegality that the act of damaging the environment is an illegal act that cannot be tolerated in the public interest, such as the preservation of the soil ecosystem and the prevention of harm to the public health and the environment, beyond the individual interests of the land owner; (2) the characteristics of land environmental pollution that are not easily revealed even when the soil is polluted and waste is buried. Thus, it is ordinary that the buyer or the subsequent buyers do not have an opportunity to rationally adjust her or their interests for the purification and treatment because she is (or they are) not aware of the environmental pollution status. Therefore, it is considered reasonable in that it cannot be entrusted to the problem of arbitration of interests between the seller responsible for environmental damage and the buyer or subsequent buyers to the transaction.

14. Supreme Court Decision 2006Da20405 Decided Jul. 26, 2007.
15. Supreme Court en banc Decision 2009Da66549 Decided May 19, 2016.

§6. PROTECTED INTERESTS

42. Article 750 of the Korean Civil Code provides that any person who causes losses to or inflicts injuries on another person by an unlawful act, intentionally or negligently, shall be bound to make compensation for damages arising therefrom. Thus, it is a comprehensive general tort provision. This approach does not enumerate the legal interests to be protected by the tort law. For example, Article 823(1) of the German Civil Code limits the legal interests to be protected by certain rights. This general tort provision was clearly intended by the legislator of the Korean Civil Code at the time of the legislation. Before the current Korean Civil Code was enacted, the Japanese Civil Code was applied in Korea when Korea was a colony of Japan for thirty-five years. At that time, the Japanese Civil Code required "infringement of rights" for tort liability because the Japanese Civil Code was influenced by the German Civil Code. However, by limiting the protection of tort law to absolute rights, this requirement made it difficult to recognize tort liability for infringement of interests that cannot be said to be property rights, such as ownership and goodwill, but are worthy of legal protection. For this reason, the legislator of the Korean Civil Code adopted the requirement of "illegal act" rather than "infringement of rights." Thus, it is not limited to the infringement of the rights of others, but if the interests to be protected legally are infringed by the illegal act, it can be regarded as tortious. It was the intention of the Korean legislator. According to the openness of the general delict provision, the scope of tort liability and the specification of the legal interests to protect are left to theories and precedents. These legal interests to protect are: (1) life, body, (2) freedom (especially physical freedom and sexual freedom), (3) property rights such as ownership, (4) rights of personality, such as honor and privacy, (5) living interests to be protected from noise and sunlight interference, and (6) business relationships and business activities, etc.

43. Life, body. It is natural that an infringement on the life of another constitutes a tortious act unless there is a separate justification for it. In relation to the protection of the survivors whose right to receive support from the victim has been violated because the victim died due to the infringement on life, there are many countries that recognize it.[16] Yet, South Korea does not have an explicit regulation on this, and according to precedents, even if the victim dies as a result of a tortious act, the deceased victim acquires the right to claim compensation for loss of lost profits, and the bereaved family receives it with the victim's death, based on inheritance.[17]

44. Infringement of the body includes not only assault or injury to the body but also infection of disease and acts of infringing health. Thus, the strict distinction

16. Article 752 of the Korean Civil Code provides that a person who has caused the death of another person shall be liable for damages to the lineal ascendants, lineal descendants, and the spouse, even where no economic damages exist as a result thereof.
17. Supreme Court Decision 66Da1335 Decided Oct. 18, 1966 (Inheritance of the right to claim non-economic damages from a deceased victim); Supreme Court Decision 69Da268 ("Even if the victim died instantly, the right to claim non-economic damages is the subject of inheritance because a time gap can be recognized between the time the victim suffered a fatal injury and death").

between bodily harm and health impairment (i.e., the former is primarily a violation of physical integrity, while the latter results in an internal or psychiatric condition) has not been raised, and damages by post-traumatic stress disorder (PTSD) have been recognized in South Korean courts. Moreover, the Supreme Court of South Korea has acknowledged compensation for damages for the second victim who witnessed the traffic accident of her older sister (8 years old at the time of the accident) and suffered from symptoms of PTSD such as mutism, sleep disturbance, childhood social withdrawal, and interpersonal impairment.[18]

The rationales of the South Korean Supreme Court were: "(1) the fact that the older sister witnessed right next to the scene where her sister was suddenly hit by a rushing car to see that her sister suffered three fractures and fractured teeth throughout her body; and (2) that the accident situation at the time was heavy and it can be fully acknowledged in terms of experience that the older sister, who was only about 9 years old at that time, must have suffered a considerable amount of psychological shock from this car accident; (3) it is medically acknowledged that the pain and mental shock from witnessing the accident can work as a "traumatic accident" and cause the onset of PTSD. It suggested that the mental stress caused by accident was significant enough to suffer. In fact, about three months after the accident, the mental stress caused by the accident was so great that the elder sister had to receive treatment for alopecia areata; (4) the results of the physical examination at the request of the first trial and the appellate court all acknowledged the relationship between the accident and the disability."

45. Freedom. The act of infringing on physical freedom by arresting or detaining others without justifiable reasons constitutes a tortious act. Activities such as driving others to be mentally ill and being admitted to a psychiatric hospital even though there are no symptoms or having a state agency arrest or detain someone who is not a criminal by accusing them are also infringing on physical freedom. In addition, infringement on the sexual freedom or right of sexual self-determination of others also constitutes a tortious act. In marital relationships (including de facto marriage), interests that can demand exclusive sexual relations between husband and wife are also considered legal interests that should be protected from infringement by third parties. Therefore, if a spouse is raped by a third party, the other spouse may be entitled to damages for the tortious act against the third-party tortfeasor.[19]

Activities that obstruct access to roads, such as public works, may also constitute tortious acts that infringe on freedom of passage. In this case, in accordance with unavoidable interchanges and the principles of free competition with others in social life, it cannot be judged as an illegal act based solely on the result of infringement. Thus, the degree of illegality of infringement, such as fraud and intimidation, should be considered.

18. Supreme Court Decision 2007Da78777 Decided Sep. 11, 2008.
19. For protection of the right to sexual self-determination, *see* further protection of interests of personality below.

46. Property Rights, including Ownership. An act that infringes on the property of another person at fault is a tortious act. Infringement of ownership does not distinguish between movable and real property. The infringement includes physical loss or damage of the property and an act that causes the loss of ownership of another person, such as in the case of passing the registration title of transfer of ownership with an invalid cause in relation to the real property of another person. In addition, since the owner can freely use and profit from the property (Article 211 of the Korean Civil Code), such as in the case of building a factory on land owned by another person without permission, infringing on the owner's usability or using the property by illegally occupying another person's property. The act of obstructing the property is also the infringement of property. The act of polluting one's own land by burying waste and selling it to a buyer without purifying the waste also constitutes a tortious act.[20]

Also, those who have usufruct rights, such as superficies, chonsegwon,[21] and lessees, have the right to receive compensation for damages if they are used or profited at fault by others. In addition, security rights, such as mortgages, are also rights that can be protected from tortious acts. For example, a bank that overestimates the value of collateral by trusting an appraiser's misinformed appraisal report and overestimates the value of collateral to make a bad loan may claim damages to the appraiser.[22]

47. Legal interests of personality rights, such as fame and privacy. The right of personality that a person has with respect to his or her personal value also falls under the legal interests protected by tort liability. Article 10 of the South Korean Constitution declares, "All citizens shall be assured of human worth and dignity." Thus, it clarifies the basis for guaranteeing the right of personality. And Article 17 of the Korean Constitution provides that the privacy of no citizen shall be infringed. Therefore, it is obvious that privacy is one of the important rights of personality to be protected. As a positive legal basis for the protection of personal rights, Articles 307 and 311 of the Korean Criminal Code on defamation and insult are provided. Article 751(1) of the Korean Civil Code provides that a person who has injured the person, liberty, or fame of another or has inflicted any mental anguish to another person shall be liable to make compensation for damages arising therefrom. In addition, Article 764 of the Korean Civil Code provides special rules applicable to defamation. It says, "The court may, on the application of the injured party, order the person who has defamed another's reputation to take measures appropriate for

---

20. Supreme Court en banc Decision 2009Da66549 Decided May 19, 2016.
21. Article 303 (Contents of Chonsegwon) of the Korean Civil Code:

> (1) Any person having chonsegwon is entitled to use it in conformity with its purposes and to take the profits from it, by paying the deposit money and possessing the real property owned by another person. Furthermore, he is also entitled to obtain the repayment of deposit money in preference to persons having the junior right or other creditors, with respect to the whole real property.

22. Supreme Court Decision 75Da2236 Decided Apr. 13, 1976; also Supreme Court Decision 99Da66618 Decided April 21.

repairing the injured party's reputation, either in lieu of, or together with provision of compensation." Regarding the infringement of reputation or other legal interests due to media reports, the Act On Press Arbitration And Damages Remedies (APADR)[23] provides detailed regulations on various remedies and procedures. Article 5(1) of the APADR defines "the right of personality as right to life, liberty, body, health, reputation, secrecy, and freedom pertaining to privacy, portrait, name, voice, dialogue, works, personal documents, any other personal worth."

48. In South Korea, protection of victims by civil tort for infringement of personal rights began to develop with the types of defamation specified in Articles 751 and 764 of the Civil Act in the 1960s and 1970s. Privacy has been protected with precedents and theories since the 1980s, and the right to commercial use such as names and portraits (so-called right of publicity) has been developed. In addition, in the protection of the right to self-determination (e.g., the violation of the patient's right to self-determination due to the violation of the doctor's duty to explain the necessity, method, side effects of medical treatment and the violation of the victim's right to sexual self-determination due to sexual harassment in the workplace), there have been tort liability issues as infringement of personality rights.[24] Furthermore, in recent years, with the development of information and communication technology, unauthorized infringement of information that can identify individuals, such as name, resident registration number, and photo, has become easier. Thus, the right to self-determination of personal information, which is an active right regarding one's own information, is also recognized as a personal right and a legal interest to be protected by the tort law. These legal interests of personality rights are treated as absolute rights that can be claimed by anyone, but as a result of the violation of personal rights, it does not constitute a tortious act by itself. Whether or not the violation of personal rights is illegal should be specifically judged on a case-by-case basis in balancing tests with opposing interests such as freedom of speech and expression and the public right to know.

49. Liability for tortious acts based on the violation of personality rights is also being used to guarantee basic constitutional rights such as religious freedom and gender equality guaranteed by the Constitution. For example, the Supreme Court of South Korea has ruled that religious education in private schools established by religious organizations is an act that infringes on the personal and legal interests of students regarding religion when it is beyond the limits that can be tolerated by common sense and legal feelings of our society.[25] In addition, if a private organization discriminates against female members for membership registration without

23. This law was enacted in 2005 and unified the media damage remedy system, which had been dispersed in individual laws such as the Act on the Registration of Periodicals, which had existed since the 1980s.
24. Supreme Court Decision 95Da39533 Decided Feb. 10, 1998; Supreme Court Decision 2016Da202947 Decided Dec. 22, 2017 (Employer's tortious liability for sexual harassment in the workplace).
25. Supreme Court en banc Decision 2008Da38288 Decided Apr. 2, 2010.

any reasonable reason and excludes female members from membership evaluation,[26] and the employer provides the same amount of work for male and female workers working within the same business, it has been judged that it constitutes an illegal act even in the case of paying a lower wage to a female worker than a male worker without a reasonable reason despite the value.

If an employer pays a female worker less than a male worker without a reasonable reason, even though the labor provided by male and female workers of the same value within the same business, they constitute tortious acts.[27]

50. Nuisance[28] infringing on the interests of living to lead a peaceful daily life, such as sunlight, noise, vibration, and view, may constitute a tortious act if it exceeds the tolerable limit in social life. Regarding the violation of living interests, such as noise and sunlight interference, the Korean Civil Code recognizes the right to claim exclusion of interference based on ownership under neighborhood relationships (Articles 214 and 217 of the Korean Civil Code) in order to stop or prevent the disturbance of living interests. To compensate for economic and non-economic damages caused by nuisance, the right to claim compensation for damages based on tortious acts is recognized. The main types of violations of the interests of living are obstruction of sunlight, noise and vibration, dust, and odors. In recent years, there has been a controversy over the infringement of the prospective interest.[29]

Nuisance, such as noise and vibration, are mainly problems in the relationship of land or buildings adjacent to each other. Legal protection against obstruction of life is recognized for those who occupy and continuously use the real estate, such as the owner of the real estate, the *cheonsei* right holder, and the lessee.

In addition, there is an unavoidable aspect of interfering with the lives of others in the process of living a social life while using one's own land or buildings. Therefore, obstruction of life can be evaluated as an offense only when it exceeds the generally tolerated limit in accordance with social norms. In a case of sunlight obstruction, the South Korean Supreme Court rules that the decision will be made by comprehensively considering all circumstances, such as the degree of damage, the nature of the damage benefit and social evaluation thereof, the use of the injured building, regionality, the precedence of land use, the possibility of damage prevention and damage avoidance, public law regulation and progress of negotiations.[30]

51. Transaction Relationships and Business Activities. The South Korean Supreme Court also recognizes tort liability under certain conditions for the

---

26. Supreme Court Decision 2009Da19864 Decided Jan. 27, 2011.
27. Supreme Court Decision 2012Da31734 Decided Jan. 16, 2013.
28. Korean Supreme Court has used the term, "living benefits" which could be from such as noise and sunlight interference.
29. The content of the view benefit that "can get rest or satisfaction while looking at a distant place" is not clear. "In principle, a certain place has a special value while looking outward from that place. One important purpose is to enjoy such prospective benefits. As in the case where a building is built on the site, it is judged to be a case where it is recognized that the view benefit that the owner or occupant enjoys from the building is so important that it should be recognized as an independent profit in accordance with social norms." Supreme Court Decision 2003Da64602 Decided Sep. 13, 2004.
30. Supreme Court Decision 2003Da64602 Decided Sep. 13, 2004.

infringement of economic damages resulting from the disruption of transaction relationships or obstruction of business activities by a third party. Some countries do not recognize liability for tort economic damages caused by infringing on pure economic damage, which is freedom of business reputation or economic activity without prejudice to the victim's absolute rights, such as life, body or ownership. However, in South Korea, Article 750 of the Korean Civil Code does not limit the legal interests of protection as long as the illegality and fault of the tortfeasor are recognized. Therefore, it is considered that pure economic damage can be protected under the Korean tort law.

However, even if transaction relationships and business activities are considered to be legal interests to be protected by tort law, infringement on other people's transaction relationships or business activities does not always constitute a tortious act.

This is because, under the market economic order, free competition activities are natural, and in the process, the consequences of violating the interests of others are inevitable. In addition, when compared to property rights such as ownership, profits from business activities and transaction relationships with others are not specific and variable and flexible depending on market conditions. Therefore, infringement on transaction relationships or business activities cannot be judged to be illegal only as a result of the infringement. The illegality of the infringing act must be actively discussed while considering the degree of infringed legal interest, the reproachability of the infringing act, and the intention of the tortfeasor. Double sales of real property, industrial action and boycott of product, economic loss due to misrepresentative information, and unfair breach of contract negotiations have mainly been dealt with in Korean cases.[31]

---

31. *See* Part I Ch. 2 §5.

Part I. Responsibility for Your Actions

Chapter 1. General Principles

§1. Unlawfulness and Fault

52. According to the general tort liability provisions of Article 750 of the Korean Civil Code, liability for damages resulting from an act inflicting harm on another person must satisfy the requirements for the illegality of the offense and intention or negligence.

The traditional opinions of Korean scholars have understood the requirement for illegality as an objective requirement and the requirement for intention or negligence as a subjective requirement.[32] The former illegality requirement is to evaluate the tortfeasor's harm as an act that goes against the norms that prohibit or order certain acts in the legal order. The latter fault is a requirement to ask whether the tortfeasor can be blamed for failing to perform an act that meets the standards required by the legal order to attribute the consequences of the harm to the person.

The Korean Civil Code does not provide for the criteria for judging illegality and intention or negligence, which are important requirements for tort liability, but leaves it to theories and precedents. Strict liability does not require the illegality, intention, or negligence of the tortious act caused by the tortfeasor.

53. Regarding the judgment of illegality, most Korean scholars have been influenced by German civil law and they have introduced two opposing approaches. One position is that the illegality of the act is presumed to be the result of infringing on a certain right or legal interest (prima facie evidence). However, when there are grounds for exclusion of illegality such as self-defense or emergency evacuation, the illegality is not recognized (Consequence illegality theory).

The other position states that illegality should be found in the act of the tortfeasor, not the result of the perpetrator. When an act that causes damage to others violates the duty of care required in social life, the illegality of the tortious act is recognized (Conduct illegality theory).[33]

According to the theory of illegal conduct, in particular, the position of judging whether or not negligence is based on objective negligence on the basis of ordinary people and average persons, there is a theoretical problem that the requirements for

32. *See* e.g., Song, Tuck-Soo, *Law of Obligations—Special Parts*, 6th ed., 528–529, Parkyoungsa, 2023.
33. Kim, Hyung-Bae, Kim, Kyu-wan & Kim, Myung-sook, *Lecture of Civil Law*, 15th ed., 1642–1643, Shinjo-sa, 2016.

negligence and negligence cannot be divided. However, Korea's dominant position is that it follows the conduct illegality theory in general, although there is also an argument to follow the consequence illegality theory in the case of directly inflicting an absolute legal interest such as the life, body, or property of another. The main reasons for this are: (1) in the case of damage caused by omission or indirect infringement, tort liability can be recognized only when the violation of the duty to prevent consequences and the occurrence of damage are recognized. (2) in the case of infringement of personality rights, living interests, or business profits, it is not possible to judge the illegality only by the result of infringement of legal interests. Therefore, the illegality can be decided according to whether the duty of care required in the relevant situation is complied with, through a balancing test between the degree of infringing legal interest, the background of the infringing act and the degree of accusation, and the opposing interests to be obtained through the infringing act. Determination of illegality based on the results of the overall evaluation of the profits and the circumstances of conduct has been a traditional position of South Korean academics influenced by Japanese civil law. According to this position, "the determination shall be made considering the legal interests being infringed and the various aspects of infringements" (correlation theory).[34]

54. It is understood that the prohibition of legal order or norms of conduct, which are the criteria for determining illegality includes not only the norms of positive law enacted and promulgated by the state but also the standards of conduct required by common social norms (the theory of substantive illegality).[35] Therefore, criminal acts contrary to the criminal law, such as injury, theft, fraud, embezzlement, etc., are recognized as illegal acts under civil liability law.

In addition, an act that violates the administrative enforcement laws stipulated by the state to maintain social order and protect the interests of the general public, in certain cases, can be evaluated as a tortious act. However, in this case, the violated law must have the purpose of directly protecting the individual from the damages that occurred in the case. This means that "the basic purpose of the entire statute, the specific purpose and content of the individual provisions imposing its obligations, the characteristics of the duties, and various circumstances such as the nature of the offending act and the degree of damage must be considered individually and specifically for determination."[36]

For example, if an employee of a securities company unfairly solicits an investment loss compensation agreement that is prohibited by the Securities Exchange Act, and the investor suffers from damages.[37] It was in violation of the ship safety

34. According to this position, there is a stage of strength and weakness between the rights or interests that are infringed. It points out that "infringement of interests with strong rights is generally more illegal than infringement of weak interests." Human behavior is divided into violations of criminal laws, violations of enforcement laws, violations of social order, and abuse of rights to determine the severity of the illegality.

35. Kim, Hyung-Bae, Kim, Kyu-wan & Kim, Myung-sook, *Lecture of Civil Law*, 15th ed., 1642, Shinjo-sa, 2016.

36. Supreme Court Decision 98Da55949 Decided Jun. 9, 2000; Supreme Court Decision 2006Da87798 Decided Jul. 23; Supreme Court Decision 2013Da41431 Decided May 28, 2015.

37. Supreme Court Decision 93Da26205 Decided Jan. 11, 1994.

regulations by overlooking the ship safety issue when conducting a ship inspection. However, a fire occurred while the vessel was operating. Passengers were injured in the fire.[38] In these cases, civil tort liabilities are recognized.

However, among the business restrictions of casino operators, the business rules that limit the one-time betting limit cannot be considered rules to prevent individual casino users from economic damage. Therefore, even if the casino users suffer economic damages due to the business in violation of the betting limit, the casino is not liable to the users for torts.[39]

The rule of conduct, which is the standard for determining illegality, includes not only positive law standards but also *naturalis ratio* rules that are individually and specifically required in the context of society in the light of popular beliefs. This duty of care is determined with a balancing test considering comprehensively the nature and content of the infringed legal interest, the background and social meaning of the infringement, and the possibility of avoiding the legal interest. According to case law in Korea, for example: (1) in the case of apartment sales, there is an obligation to notify the other party in the contract negotiation process about important matters in forming the contract;[40] (2) the duty to act in order to recognize the tortious act caused by the omission that did not prevent the tortious act of the direct tortfeasor.[41] They have been recognized as an unwritten duty of care in the comprehensive balancing tests. Furthermore, in the case of information providers (website operators) who collect and disclose information, such as the lawyer's network index, win rates and professionalism index, without the consent of the lawyers.[42] It is ruled that even in the case of infringement of personal legal interests, such as personal information infringement, the illegality can be determined only by a balancing test.

55. The South Korean literature introduces the specific contents of the illegality judgment by dividing them into types of infringed legal interests and infringing actions based on a general and theoretical approach to judgment of illegality. For example, the types of infringed legal interests include: (1) life and body, (2) freedom (especially physical freedom and sexual freedom), (3) property rights such as ownership, (4) rights of personality such as honor and privacy, (5) life interest to be protected from noise and obstruction of sunlight, (6) transaction relationship and business activity. In the case of absolute legal interests such as (1), (2), and (3), illegality is generally not a problem if damage is recognized as a violation of rights. However, as in (4), (5), and (6), if the protection content of the right is not clear or it is only a relative right, courts explain the illegality of the offense by balancing the background of the offense and the degree of reproachability, the degree and probability of infringement of legal interests, and profits through infringement. Regarding the form of infringement, South Korean literature and precedents provide legal principles on the forms of tortious acts resulting from abuse of rights, such as: (1)

38. Supreme Court Decision 91Da43466 Decided Feb. 12, 1993.
39. Supreme Court en banc Decision 2010Da92438 decided Aug. 21, 2014.
40. Supreme Court Decision 2005Da5843 decided Jun. 1, 2007.
41. Supreme Court Decision 2010Da8709 decided Apr. 26, 2012.
42. Supreme Court en banc Decision 2008Da42430 decided Sep. 2, 2011.

tortious acts by omission,[43] (2) tortious acts resulting from violation of official duties, such as of public servants,[44] and (3) tortious acts of right of abuse, such as unfair dismissal and unfair lawsuits.[45]

§2. Concept of Fault

56. The principle of negligence.

Article 750 of the Korean Civil Code stipulates that any person who causes losses to or inflicts injuries on another person by an unlawful act, intentionally or negligently, shall be bound to make compensation for damages arising therefrom. Article 390 of the Korean Civil Code also sets the condition of liability for the obligor's intention or negligence in breach of contract. The principle of fault liability is regarded as one of the three fundamental principles along with the principle of freedom of contract and respect for ownership in the Korean Civil Law. By adopting the principle of responsibility for negligence, the Korean civil law attempts to guarantee the freedom of individual actions, which is inevitable in social life, providing the principle that "those who are not at fault are not responsible for damages." However, with the development of mass transportation and science and technology, the risk factors beyond human control are constantly increasing in South Korea. Thus, even before the enactment of the Korean Civil Code, the no-fault liability without asking whether an individual was at fault was legislated by individual laws.[46] Liability of Possessor, Owner of Structure in the Korean Civil Code is stipulated as strict liability. (Article 758(1)).[47]

57. Intention and negligence. In principle, civil tort liability is recognized even if there is negligence, unlike criminal liability based on intention. Therefore, the distinction between intention and negligence in establishing tort liability has no special meaning, and the scope of damages does not, in principle, vary depending on intention and negligence. However, there are individual cases where the degree of reproachability or negligence is considered in determining the scope of damages compensation. For example, the South Korean Supreme Court has already considered the degree of malice in the overall libel advertisements in calculating the amount of damages caused by libel advertisements between competing companies in the 1990s.[48] In the "Appropriate Compensation Calculation Method for Each Type of Tortious Acts" announced in 2017, it is stipulated that non-economic damages can be aggravated according to the intention of the tortfeasor and the degree of

43. *See* Part I Ch. 1 §3.
44. *See* Part I Ch. 2 §2.
45. *See* Part I Ch. 2 §3.
46. For example, in Art. 60(1) of the Mining Act enacted in 1951, the liability for compensation for mine damage is stipulated regardless of the intentional or negligence of the mining right holder.
47. (1) If any damages have been caused to another person by reason of any defect in the construction or maintenance of a structure, the person in possession of the structure shall be liable for such damages: Provided, That if the person in possession has exercised due care in order to prevent the occurrence of such damages, compensation for the damage shall be made by the owner.
48. Supreme Court Decision 93Da40614, 40621 decided Apr. 12, 1996.

reproachability for certain types of harm. In addition, in the cases of certain harmful acts, Article 35 of the Fair Transactions in Subcontracting Act, Article 13 of the Act on The Protection, etc., of Fixed-term And Part-time Employees, and Article 3 of the Product Liability Act provide that a certain multiple is added to the actual damage of the victim to compensate the victim. These Special Acts consider the maliciousness of the tortfeasor as a weighting factor in the case of liability for damages.

58. Intention. Intention refers to a state of being willing to do something while recognizing the consequences of infringing on the rights or legal interests of others. In other words, the possibility of intentional reproach is found in the awareness and will to infringe on the rights or interests of others. Intention is recognized not only when the actor knows that the consequences of harm will occur through his or her actions but also when he/she considers the consequences to be possible and accepts unavoidable consequences (*dolus eventualis*). According to the South Korean Supreme Court, what the tortfeasor has to be aware of in order to satisfy the requirement for intention is limited to the occurrence of the consequences of infringement of rights or legal interests. Therefore, there is no need for the tortfeasor to be aware of the illegality of his or her actions.[49] Most South Korean scholars agree with the Supreme Court. The majority theory states that civil liability for damages does not require a separate recognition of the illegality because the purpose is not to punish the tortfeasor but rather to be liable for the damages equitably.[50]

59. Negligence. Negligence refers to a state in which the actor neglected to pay attention even though he could have known that he was infringing on the rights or interests of others if he had been careful. In other words, the reproachability of negligence lies in the acknowledgement and foreseeability of the infringement of the rights or interests of others. In relation to the standard of attention required for determining negligence, in South Korea, some scholars argue that the duty of care of the individual who infringed protected legal interests should be the standard (subjective negligence theory). However, the major opinion of legal scholars and cases in South Korea have taken the duty of care that can be expected to be observed in social life from the average person or, more precisely, the average person in the occupation or situation to which the tortfeasor belongs (objective negligence theory). Therefore, for example, even if a doctor commits a medical malpractice that cannot be blamed under his subjective circumstances, if he fails to observe the objectively required medical rules, he is liable for the medical malpractice. South Korean precedents and most legal scholars have adopted objective negligence to consider the purpose and function of civil liability to protect social trust and equitable sharing of damage despite differences in individual duty of care.[51]

Negligence includes the possibility of acknowledging and avoiding infringement of rights or interests. Both acknowledgment and avoidability are required, and

49. Supreme Court Decision 2001Da46440, decided Jul. 12, 2002.
50. *See* Lee, Yeon-gap, *The Commentary of Korean Civil Code—Law of Obligations (6)*, 140, 2022.
51. *See* Lee, Yeon-gap, *The Commentary of Korean Civil Code—Law of Obligations (6)*, 143–145, 2022.

whether the possibility of acknowledging an infringement of the legal interests of others should be objectively judged in consideration of the occupation in which the actor belongs and the characteristics of the given situation. For example, those who perform blood management tasks must pay high attention to anticipating and avoiding even the slightest risk in advance in order to keep the purity of blood, protect donors and recipients, and ensure proper blood management.[52] In contrast, a negligent violation of a school teacher's duty to supervise a minor student is recognized only when it is predicted or could have been predicted that an accident by the supervised would normally occur, that is, when there is a specific risk.[53]

Furthermore, negligence is a factor of the possibility in which the tortfeasor can avoid the infringement of legal interests of others. In this respect, a distinction is made between negligence and strict liability. However, the judgment of the possibility of avoidance includes not only the actual possibility that the actor could actually avoid the infringement of legal interests but also the normative factors regarding whether it is expected that he should have avoided the infringement of legal interests according to social norms. Accordingly, the higher the degree of the duty of care to prevent the foreseeable infringement of legal interests, the more the negligence liability functions as a strict liability close to the strict liability. Furthermore, negligence is a factor in the possibility of avoidance of legal interests by the perpetrator, and in this respect, negligence and risk liability are distinguished. However, the judgment of the possibility of avoidance includes not only the actual possibility that the actor could actually avoid the infringement of legal interests but also the normative element regarding whether it is expected that he should have avoided the infringement of legal interests according to the social convention, and thus as the degree of due diligence to prevent predictable infringement of legal interests is increased, the negligence liability functions as a strict liability close to the risk liability. In principle, negligence is an abstract negligence based on the normal duty of care required of ordinary people. Therefore, the tort liability under Article 750 of the Korean Civil Code is sufficient as an abstract negligence of the tortfeasor.

However, the subjective requirements for establishing responsibility may be determined by gross negligence according to legal provisions[54] or agreement of the parties. Gross negligence refers to a case in which the actor has significantly neglected the duty of care required by social norms. However, the Korean Civil Code lowers the duty of care by breaking away from the strict objective and abstract negligence principle in cases such as the custody of bailed items by the gratuitous bailee and the management of property of the children in of parental authority.[55] In these cases, while using the expression "the same degree of care … with respect to his own property," the actor is liable for damages depending on whether he is negligent in the specific situation.

52. Supreme Court Decision 94Da47803, decided Aug. 25, 1995.

53. Supreme Court Decision 96Da44433, decided Jun. 13, 1995.

54. *See* for example, Arts. 401 and 735 of the Korean Civil Code; Art. 401 of the Korean Commercial Code, and Art. 2, para. 2 of the Korean State Compensation Act.

55. *See* Arts. 695, 922 and 1022 of the Korean Civil Code.

60. Burden of Proof.

In principle, the burden of proving the tortfeasor's intention or negligence is borne by the victim who asks him for compensation for damages. However, in certain cases, the burden of proof is shifted to the tortfeasor or the tortfeasor's negligence is factually presumed. In the case of the supervisor's responsibility for a minor or person of mental unsoundness under Article 755 of the Korean Civil Code and the employer's responsibility for the employee's actions under Article 756 of the Civil Code, the supervisor or employer who is obligated to compensate may be exempted from liability by proving that he or she has not neglected his or her supervisory duty. In addition, precedents have eased the victim's burden of proof by establishing legal theories of de facto estimating the tortfeasor's negligence from certain indirect facts based on empirical rules in some types of harmful acts, such as medical malpractice[56] and environmental pollution.

§3. Duty of Care

61. In South Korea's tort liability, the duty of care plays an important role in filtering whether liability is established (especially by negligence). This is because, although the duty of care is stipulated as an independent requirement for establishing responsibility or as a component, it recognizes the illegality and responsibility of infringement of legal interests when there is a breach of the duty of care.

62. The content of the duty of care may be specifically stipulated in the provisions of the positive law. For example, the Road Traffic Act, the Police Officer's Duty Execution Act on the Use of Firearms, and the Safety Management Act on the Handling and Transport of Dangerous Substances are legal provisions that can be considered for the specification of the duty of care. In addition, the rules of business handling established in the case of certain professions, such as doctors, lawyers, and certified public accountants (e.g., accounting audit rules in the case of certified public accountants) are also important factors to consider in determining the duty of care. Practices may also be considered. However, even in the case of an act according to the custom, if the practice itself does not meet the normatively required, a breach of the duty of care cannot be exempt.[57] Ultimately, the content and degree of the duty of care have the character of a general clause that must be specified by the judge in each individual situation. Therefore, the determination should be made with the balancing test of guarantee of freedom of action in the potential tortfeasor's position and of protection of rights and interests in the victim's position.

In determining the balancing test, the necessity to protect the right or legal interest at risk, the social value of the potentially harmful act, the probability of occurrence of damage, and the expectation of avoidance of damage should be comprehensively considered. Therefore, the higher the value of the legal interests at

56. *See* Part I Ch. 2 §1 II.

57. Supreme Court Decision 97Do2812, decided Feb. 27, 1998 (a criminal case due to medical malpractice).

risk of infringement and the higher the size and probability of damage to occur, the stricter the duty of care is required for the tortfeasors.

63. The content of the duty of care to foresee and avoid the infringement of the rights or legal interests of others may be specifically determined according to the occupation of the actor and the area of the relevant act. A higher duty of care is required in situations where there is a risk of harming legal interests with high social value, such as the life and body of others. Persons belonging to certain professions, such as doctors and lawyers, are required to have the professional knowledge and ability generally expected of the professional in performing their professional activities. However, the degree of request for duty of care should be judged in consideration of the individual circumstances in which the infringement has occurred. For example, if a patient visits a small rural hospital in an emergency to receive his or her medical treatment, the medical standard of a large medical institution in a large city with advanced medical facilities cannot be expected in this case.[58]

64. The duty of care can be individually specified by the judge in the situation of infringement of legal interests. It can exist not only in the form of an obligation not to actively inflict harm on the rights and interests of others but also in the form of an obligation to act to prevent risks to the protection and legal interests of others. However, this duty of care to prevent risks shall not be easily recognized. According to the South Korean Supreme Court, the principle of good faith, social norms, or duty on nature of things are special trust relationships due to kinship or contractual relationships, or, in the position of controlling or managing a risk factor that may cause damage to the other party, or in a position to supervise the actions of others, it is recognized that the person has the responsibility to take measures to prevent damage from the risk factors or the actions of others under individual and specific circumstances. Only those who have a special position to protect the other party's legal interests or prevent infringement on their legal interests are recognized.[59]

§4. Ability (Child, Person of Mental Unsoundness)

65. According to Article 753 of the Korean Civil Code, if a minor who is a person under the age of 19, Article 4 of the Korean Civil Code, inflicts damage on another person, there is no liability for damages if the person was not in possession of sufficient intelligence to understand his responsibility for the act. In addition, according to Article 754 of the Korean Civil Code, while in a state of mental unsoundness, a person who has caused damage to another is not liable for damages resulting therefrom.[60] According to the South Korean dominant view, children and persons of mental unsoundness cannot be blamed for the reproachability of fault

58. Supreme Court Decision 86Daka2095, decided Sep. 8, 1987.
59. Supreme Court Decision 2010Da8709, decided Apr. 26, 2012.
60. That this shall not be the case, if he has brought upon himself his state of mental unsoundness either intentionally or negligently.

against the actors who assume the foreseeability and avoidability of infringement of legal interests. The burden of proof as to whether or not a person is liable shall be borne by the person claiming immunity on the basis of incapacity.

66. According to Article 753 of the Korean Civil Code, the capacity to be responsible refers to the intelligence or ability to judge the responsibility of a tortious act according to one's own actions.

In some countries, it is expressly stipulated that persons under a certain age (e.g., 7 years of age) have no responsibility at all, but the Korean Civil Code stipulates that individual judgments should be made after considering the risk of the infringement situation and other factors.

However, according to precedent, generally, responsibility is not recognized under the age of 12. However, there is a tendency to recognize responsibility for minors over the age of 15. In addition, for those who are 13–14 years old, specific judgments are made on a case-by-case basis. Whether or not there is a capacity for liability is treated differently from the capacity for acknowledgement necessary for comparative negligence. Therefore, the capacity for comparative negligence can be recognized even for children who are considered not to have the capacity for liability.

67. A person who is unable to take responsibility due to mental unsoundness is a person who lacks normal judgment ability due to incapacity or mental illness. Whether or not the person is of mental unsoundness must be specifically determined based on the time of the tortious act. Therefore, even though a person has not been adjudicated for the commencement of adult guardianship, if the person is in a state of mental unsoundness, he or she is recognized as not liable for damages under Article 754 of the Korean Civil Code. However, even though a person has been adjudicated to commence adult guardianship due to continued mental unsoundness, if he or she temporarily returns to a normal mental state at the time of the act, he or she is recognized as a person with capacity to take responsibility.

68. According to Articles 753 and 754 of the Korean Civil Code, if a child or a person who is in a state of mental unsoundness is not liable for the damage caused by them, the supervisor who has a statutory duty for them under Article 755 of the Civil Code is liable for the damage. However, the liability of the supervisor follows the principle of negligence. Therefore, if the supervisor proves that he or she has not neglected his or her duty of supervision, he or she is not liable for damages. In such cases, some countries may provide for equitable compensation for those who are incapable of taking responsibility for the protection of victims. However, the Korean Civil Code does not provide for such equitable liability in order to adhere to the principle of negligence. In the cases where minors are incapable of liability causes, there have been very a few judgments in which the liability for damages is denied on the ground that the parental authority has violated the duty of supervision.

Chapter 2. Specific Cases of Liability

§1. Liability of Professionals

I. General: High Standard of Care for Experts

69. According to the division of labor and the specialization of society, the expression "professional responsibility" is often used in South Korea to indicate the special duty of care necessary for professional activities. Professionals: (1) receive long-term, high-level education and training according to the professionalism and specificity of their work; (2) receive social recognition and trust according to the license system; (3) The contents of their vocational activities have a large impact on the public interest as well as the private interests of customers. Therefore, they bear a high duty of care in performing their duties. Not to be misunderstood, the imposition of such a high degree of care on professional professionals does not imply that there is a distinct category of professional responsibility distinct from the general public. It merely reflects the general thinking regarding the embodiment of the duty of care, that is, "the duty of care is embodied according to what is generally expected to be observed in the performance of the job of the worker of the profession to which the actor belongs." Therefore, a professional must possess the professional skills and abilities possessed by the occupational worker in which he or she is engaged. Therefore, if an individual actor does not meet these objective standards in the performance of his or her duties, he or she cannot avoid responsibility for negligence.

70. Civil liability that an expert bears by inflicting damage to others through negligence in performing his or her duties can be divided into the relationship between the client and a third party. In relation to the client, the expert will usually perform his or her duties according to the contractual relationship with the client. Therefore, in the case of negligence inflicting damage to the client in the course of performing his or her duties, he or she shall be liable for the breach of contract. However, if, for example, in the case of medical negligence, the violation of the professional's obligations also satisfies the liability requirements of Article 750 of the Korean Civil Code, the tort liability may be recognized competitively. Meanwhile, in relation to a third party that is not in a contractual relationship, the expert bears the tort liability for the damage of the third party if the duty to protect the life, body, and property of the third party is recognized. However, in a relationship with a third party that is not in a contractual relationship, the expert bears the tort liability for the damage of the third party as long as the duty to protect the life, body, and property of the third party is recognized. Below, we will introduce the duty of care of some professionals, such as doctors and lawyers.

II. Medical Malpractice

71. Medical malpractice in general.

Civil liability for medical malpractice means liability for damages for accidents caused by the negligence of doctors or other medical personnel during medical practice. Liability for medical malpractice, one of the types of civil liability that is frequently problematic, can be composed of liability for breach of contract, as medical acts are usually performed according to medical contracts with patients. The medical malpractice may be charged with tort liability for illegal, faulty infringements on life or body of others without the contractual relationship. Although South Korean scholars have supported the contractual liability of medical malpractice, South Korean courts have taken it mainly with tort liability liability.[61] The liability for breach of contract is advantageous to the creditor, who is the victim, in terms of the burden of proof on the intention and negligence of the tortfeasor, compared to the composition of the original tort liability. However, this point does not work in medical malpractice.

According to the proviso to Article 390 of the Korean Civil Code, in the case of a breach of contract, the obligor is to be exempted by proving that there is no intention or negligence. To this extent, the liability for breach of contract is advantageous to the creditor, who is the victim, compared to the tort liability. However, the creditor, who is the victim and who wants to ask for malpractice, has to prove the fact that the medical personnel violated the contract, that is, "incomplete performance" and that the medical treatment was not properly performed. This means that the creditor, who is the victim, has to prove the medical personnel's negligence of not paying attention. Therefore, in civil liability for medical malpractice, the composition of contract liability and tort liability do not differ significantly in terms of the burden of proof for the intention or negligence of the medical personnel who are the tortfeasors. Rather, that tort liability is recognized for compensation for non-economic damage to lineal ascendants, lineal descendants and the spouse, other than direct victims due to medical malpractice in accordance with Article 752 of the Korean Civil Code, compared to the liability for breach of contract, which is limited to the protection of the contracting parties. Thus, it is considered that the tort liability may be advantageous for the protection of the victim. Medical malpractice is divided into two types in South Korea. First, the basic type is liability for violating the duty of care required of medical personnel in the course of medical practice. The second is the responsibility for violating the duty to explain certain matters to the patient in addition to the provision of medical services. Civil liability for medical malpractices of oriental doctors,[62] pharmacists,[63] and midwives[64] is also a problem, but we will focus on the doctors below.

72. Responsibility for medical malpractice. Medical personnel perform medical activities such as examination and treatment, and they have a high duty of care to take the best measures required to prevent risks according to the specific symptoms or circumstances of the patient, according to the characteristics of the job that manages human life, body, and health. The standard for determining the negligence of medical personnel or duty of care is based on objective negligence, as in cases of

61. *See* Kim, Cheon-Su, *The Commentary of Korean Civil Code—Law of Obligations (6)*, 523–528, 2022.
62. Supreme Court Decision 2001Da56904, decided Dec. 10, 2002.
63. Supreme Court Decision 2001Da277449, decided Jan. 11, 2002.
64. Supreme Court Decision 2006Da79520, decided May 27, 2010.

other civil liability. According to precedents and theories in South Korea, medical practices should be judged based on the level of medical practice done in the medical clinical institutions at that time.[65]

With respect to the time and circumstances that serve as the criteria for negligence, the time at which the medical treatment in question was performed is taken as the standard. Therefore, medical personnel bear the obligation to constantly strive to keep up with the development and change of medical technology. In addition, the circumstances under which the medical treatment was performed should be taken into account. In particular, the necessity and urgency of medical treatment play an important role in determining the duty of care. For example, the doctor's duty of care should be judged differently in the treatment of an urgent disease and in the case of non-urgent cosmetic surgery.[66] However, the objective criterion for determining whether the medical practice was negligent is the level of medical practice done in the field of clinical medicine at the time of the medical practice. That is, it is based on common medical knowledge that is generally widely known and recognized by ordinary doctors through standard textbooks and other medical literature at the time of treatment. In addition, it is based on practical clinical medicine applied to patients, not on the academic level of medical care.[67] Also, the difference between the treatment environment and medical facilities should be considered a criterion for determining the duty of care. General hospitals such as university hospitals are superior to small private hospitals in terms of human and physical facilities of medical institutions, so they generally require a higher level of medical practice. The level of medical care required for the average medical person will be the standard for negligence. At this time, the grades of medical institutions and individual doctors must also be considered. Therefore, experts are expected to have higher professional knowledge and skills compared to non-specialists in their field of expertise. Therefore, a specialist and a non-specialist cannot equate the degree to the judgment of the duty of care.[68]

Medical errors are broadly divided into two stages: diagnosis and treatment. The duty of care in diagnosis is the duty to be careful not to misdiagnose by faithfully conducting examinations, since it may be directly related to negligence in medical treatment such as selection of treatment methods. Regarding the determination of diagnostic negligence, the South Korean Supreme court said, "In determining whether diagnostic negligence exists, it is impossible to conduct a perfect clinical diagnosis in the process. However, at least within the scope of the diagnostic level practiced in the field of clinical medicine, the doctor needs carefully to examine and accurately diagnose the patient according to the medical ethics and medical knowledge and experience required as a professional, predicting the occurrence of dangerous results and the occurrence of the results, so that he or she would exercise the best care necessary to avoid them. In addition, if the examination necessary for diagnosis cannot be performed due to the facilities of the medical institution, geographical factors, and other various circumstances, the doctor recommends that the

65. Supreme Court Decision 2007Da75396, decided Apr. 10, 2008.
66. Supreme Court Decision 94Da27151, decided Apr. 25, 1995.
67. Supreme Court Decision 98Da12270, decided Jul. 24, 1998.
68. Supreme Court Decision 98Da21403, decided Nov. 23, 1999.

patient be transferred to the relevant medical institution so that the patient can receive the test, unless there are special circumstances. Therefore, the doctor has such a duty to do it."[69]

However, the duty of care in treatment is to use one's own professional knowledge and skills in the process of administration, injection, surgery, anesthesia, and blood transfusion for the treatment of diseases revealed in the diagnostic act, so as not to cause harm to the patient. Surgical medical negligence includes the necessity of surgery or the wrong selection of the surgical time, the wrong choice of the surgical method, the wrong surgical technique or procedure, and the negligence of patient management after surgery.

73. The burden of proof of negligence and causation. Civil liability for medical malpractice is conditional on the negligence of medical personnel and the causal relationship (between negligent medical treatment and damage). The burden of proof shall be borne by the victim who intends to claim damages. However, according to the professionalism, discretion, and confidentiality of the medical practice, it is very difficult for the victim to prove the negligence and causal relationship of the medical personnel. Accordingly, South Korean courts have formulated the following rules to alleviate the victim's burden of proof in case of medical malpractice:

> In order to be held liable for a tort or a breach of the duty of care in medical practice, a causal relationship must exist between the breach of the duty of care in medical practice and the occurrence of damage. However, medical practice is a field that requires highly specialized knowledge, and the medical process can only be known by the doctor (except the patient may know small parts in most cases). Medical techniques to achieve the outcome of treatment are at the discretion of the physician. Therefore, it is impossible to find out whether the direct cause of the damage is caused by medical negligence by an ordinary person who is not a professional doctor. Therefore, it is extremely difficult for the patient to prove perfectly medically the causal relationship between the physician's breach of the duty of care in medical practice and the occurrence of damage. When a patient dies during the medical treatment, the victim's side may prove medical negligence based on common sense committed in the course of a series of medical practices, (e.g., the fact that the patient did not have a health defect that could cause such an outcome prior to the medical practice), the medical personnel have to prove that the result was not due to their medical malpractice, but that there may be other intervening causes.
>
> Therefore, for victims, it would alleviate the burden of proof so that the liability for damages could be assumed by estimating a causal relationship between medical negligence and results. It would be harmonized with the ideal of the damage compensation system, which guides the fair and reasonable burden of damages.[70]

69. Supreme Court Decision 97Da38442, decided Feb. 27, 1998.
70. Supreme Court Decision 93Da52402, decided Feb. 10, 1995.

According to this, in medical malpractice, the victim still bears the burden of proof for the negligent treatment of the medical personnel. However, it is not strictly medically necessary to assert or prove the fact of violation of the medical standards to be applied in the relevant treatment. Rather, it is enough to assert points that are inconceivable in light of common sense.[71] In addition, if the medical practitioner's negligence is proven to this extent, as long as the victim asserts and proves that no other cause (e.g., the patient's health defect) can be intervened between the results of the harm except a series of medical actions, negligent medical practice and a causal relationship between the occurrence of damage is presumed. Therefore, unless the medical personnel disprove this, the medical personnel bear the responsibility to compensate for the damage. South Korean scholars further argue that the burden of proof should be shifted in cases where there is a high possibility of accusation of medical personnel, such as when a serious negligence of a medical professional is proven or when medical professionals obstruct a patient to prove their medical malpractice.

74. Duty of explanation and its contents. Doctors are obliged to explain important matters related to the patient's treatment, such as the type and contents of the disease, treatment methods, and accompanying risks to the patient or the patient's guardian. As long as the medical contract is premised, the doctor's duty to explain is recognized as an obligation incidental to the medical duty, which is the main contractual obligation. However, the doctor's duty to explain is recognized without considering whether a medical contract exists. In case of violation of the duty of explanation, medical personnel shall bear the tort liability. According to one view, the basis for the recognition of the duty of explanation in tort liability is that it is itself illegal for a doctor to infringe on a patient's body in the course of medical treatment. For this reason, such illegality can be excluded only when the patient has received his or her doctor's explanation and consented to the treatment of the doctor. Contrary to this traditional position, there is a recent view that the duty of explanation is to protect the patient's right to personality or self-determination. In other words, patients have the right to choose whether to receive a medical treatment and how to have it. Therefore, if the doctor does not properly explain the need for the medical treatment, risks, and sequelae in the course of treatment, it is an act of infringing on the patient's right to self-determination. According to the recent view, the neglect of the doctor's duty of explanation is evaluated as an act that violates legal interests of the patient's right to know and self-determination. Therefore, in principle, the doctor is liable for non-economic damages to the patient. The doctor's duty of explanation applies to cases that require the patient to make a choice based on the right to self-determination, such as in the process of inflicting his or her body, such as surgery, medical practice that is likely to cause bad results or medical practice in which serious consequences such as death are predicted. The

71. In other cases in South Korea regarding medical malpractice, there are cases where the de facto presumption of negligence was developed. For example, according to the Supreme Court Decision 83Daka1350, decided Nov. 22, 1983, in the case of paralysis of the left lower after surgery, when all other possibilities, such as the patient's specific diathesis, are not considered to be the cause of the paralysis except in the case of inflicting damage during the operation. The Supreme Court held that the doctor's negligence is presumed.

subject of the duty of explanation is, in principle, the treating doctor, but explanations through the attending physician or other doctors may be permitted.[72] The other party is the patient himself. However, if the patient himself does not have the ability to judge or there are special circumstances that prevent direct explanation, the doctor can explain it to a representative. The doctor must explain the patient's symptoms, the content and degree of the infringement, such as surgery, the prospect of treatment, such as surgery, the necessity and urgency of the infringement, the symptoms in case of no treatment, other treatment methods, the consequences and expected consequences of the infringement risk, etc. Of course, the doctor's duty to explain may be restricted or exempted in case of an urgent situation and there is no time to obtain the patient's consent or if the explanation adversely affects the patient or adversely affects medical care.[73]

In relation to the burden of proof on whether or not the duty of explanation has been violated, the South Korean Supreme Court held, "the duty of explanation is a procedural measure that is essential for doctors in the process of proceeding to medical practice of characteristic of infringement. In light of the importance of the duty to explain, there is a need for doctors to at least document and preserve the explanations to the patient. While it is very easy for a doctor to prove fulfillment of the duty of explanation by such documents, it is extremely difficult to prove that the duty of explanation has not been fulfilled on the part of the patient. Considering these points, unless there are special circumstances, the doctor has the burden of proving that it has fulfilled its duty of explanation."[74]

75. Contents of compensation for breach of duty of explanation. There is a debate as to whether the scope of liability for compensation for damages caused by a doctor's violation of explanation is limited to non-economic damage or includes all damages, including economic damage. South Korean courts have recognized only non-economic damages or all damage, including economic damages caused by bodily harm, depending on the specific content and degree of violation of the duty of explanation in individual cases. The South Supreme Court held a case in which a doctor performed an operation in violation of his duty of explanation, and the patient was dead in the process of the operation, " If the patient claims only compensation for the loss of the opportunity to choose and the inability to exercise the right to self-determination, it is sufficient to prove the fact that the opportunity to choose is lost due to the doctor's lack of explanation. Also, there is no need to prove the casual relationship that the death or other consequences would not have occurred if the explanation had been received. However, in the case of claiming all damages resulting from the result, there must be a significant causal relationship between the serious result and the violation of the doctor's duty to explain or an error in the process of obtaining consent. In that case, the violation of the physician's duty of explanation is equivalent to the violation of the physician's duty of care required in the process of medical infringement on the patient's life or body in

72. Supreme Court Decision 99Da10479, decided Sep. 3, 1999.
73. Supreme Court Decision 96Da37862, decided Jul. 22, 1997.
74. Supreme Court Decision 2005Da5867, decided May 31, 2007.

light of the point to protect the patient's right to self-determination and the opportunity to choose his or her medical treatment."

76. Expansion of the subject of liability. Responsibility for medical malpractice is borne by the treating physician. In the case of joint treatment in which several doctors jointly treat a patient, the negligent practitioner is responsible for the doctor's independence and discretion. However, if it is impossible to reveal who the negligent medical practitioner is, all medical doctors are jointly liable for tortious acts (Article 760(2) of the Korean Civil Code). However, when joint medical treatment is in a relationship between a supervisor and an assistant, such as between a primary doctor and a trainee, the doctor, as the supervisor, is also responsible for violation of the supervisory duty for the negligence of the doctor in the position of assistant. In case of negligence of medical assistants, such as nurses and medical technicians, doctors who direct and supervise them shall bear the employer's responsibility (Article 756 of the Korean Civil Code) or the liability for breach of contract (Articles 391[75] and 390 of the Korean Civil Code). Independent responsibility may also be recognized if there is a violation of the doctor's duty to direct and supervise medical assistants. Business owners who hire doctors are also liable for the negligence of doctors. Furthermore, in the case of a medical accident due to a defect in the medical device, the doctor may also be liable for medical malpractice, except in cases where there is no expectation for the doctor to discover the defect.

77. Medical Dispute Mediation and Arbitration System. In South Korea, in 2012, by stipulating matters related to dispute settlement procedures and compensation for damages caused by medical accidents in 2012, "the Act on Remedies for Injuries from Medical Malpractice and Mediation of Medical Disputes" was introduced. The purpose of this Act is to quickly relieve the damage caused by medical accidents and to create a stable treatment environment for health and medical personnel. The main contents of this Act are: (1) establishment of the South Korea Medical Dispute Mediation Agency whose main tasks are mediation and arbitration of medical disputes, appraisal of medical accidents, calculation of damages and payment for damages, (2) exceptions for criminal punishment, (3) voluntary precondition of mediation for patients to give autonomous decision-making rights for mediation options, (4) introduction of a mediation period of up to three months, and (5) implementation of a no-fault medical accident compensation system in case of childbirth caused by force majeure where the doctor is not at fault. Mediation procedures for medical disputes can be initiated only when the respondent agrees to mediation with respect to the applicant's request. However, in the event of a serious medical accident, such as death, which is the subject of the application for mediation, mediation procedures must be initiated regardless of the respondent's consent.

75. Article 391 (Intention or Negligence of Performance Assistant):

> Where a legal representative for the obligor effects performance in lieu of the latter or the obligor effects performance through the other person as an employee, the intention or negligence of the legal representative or the other person shall be deemed as that of the obligor.

III. Malpractice of Legal Practitioners

78. Lawyers' Civil Liability in General. Compared to the number of lawsuits for civil liability against lawyers in the United States and Germany, the number in South Korea is significantly smaller. The reasons for this are: (1) the mistakes of lawyers have been corrected in advance according to the role of guardianship, such as the exercise of the right of clarification by the court; (2) the fact that it is difficult for ordinary people to find the negligence of lawyers because the work of lawyers is professional and intangible; (3) the number of lawyers is relatively small. Therefore, the social status of lawyers is high. Also, it is not easy to find an attorney who can file a lawsuit against a fellow lawyer. In addition, although there is a private aspect that lawyers represent clients' affairs as free professionals, there is also a social perception that they perform public duties for the realization of social justice. Therefore, this perception is considered to contribute to less contention of civil responsibility against lawyers.

The Attorney-at-law Act is enacted with respect to the qualifications, duties and rights of lawyers. The legal composition of a lawyer's civil liability is divided into a relationship to a client and a relationship to a third party. In relation to the client, the contractual liability, according to the mandate contract[76] between the lawyer and the client, is an issue. In addition, in the case of damage caused to a third party due to the actions of the lawyer, the tort liability is recognized.

79. Attorney's Duty of Care. In the relationship with the client, the lawyer is obliged to handle the duties with the care of a good manager in the position of the mandatary. In other words, lawyers, as legal experts, are obliged to deal with the matter objectively and in the best possible way based on their expertise. A lawyer's duty of prudence depends on the area and stage of the lawyer's work: (1) the duty to clearly understand the facts in the client's case, (2) the duty to investigate and study the legal relationship in the case, (3) the duty to take appropriate procedural measures necessary for the proceeding of the trial, and (4) the duty to counsel and to advice to the client, (5) the duty to notify and report important matters to the client, and (6) the duty of confidentiality. In South Korea, there are many cases of negligence in procedural measures in the trial process, where the error of lawyers is a relatively obvious type. The South Korean Supreme Court has recognized the civil liability of lawyers in the following cases: both sides fail to appear at the appeals court twice, the appeal is considered to be withdrawn and the client is defeated;[77] a judgment in defeat is finalized on the client by causing the litigation to pass the period for filing an appeal;[78] the appeal is dismissed because the lawyer in charge

76. Article 680 (Definition of Mandate) of the Korean Civil Code:

> A mandate shall become effective when one of the parties has entrusted the other party with the management of affairs and the other party has consented thereto.

77. Supreme Court Decision 4292Minsang271, decided Nov. 26, 1959.
78. Supreme Court Decision 96Da36289, decided Dec. 10, 1996.

of the appeal did not submit a statement of grounds of the final civil appeal even after the deadline for submission of the reason for appeal has passed.[79]

In addition, lawyers are obliged to be careful not to inflict unreasonable damage on third parties in handling entrusted affairs. There have been a small number of cases regarding lawyers' liability to third parties. Attorneys must check the client's personal information accurately to deal with their business. The South Korean Supreme Court recognized the civil liability of the lawyer in a case where a third party suffered economic damage while trusting the real estate registration of real forged documents, which were neglected by the lawyer.[80]

80. Professional Responsibilities of Certified Judicial Scriveners in South Korea, besides lawyers, there are legal professionals called "Certified Judicial Scriveners." A Certified Judicial Scrivener acts on behalf of others in the preparation of documents submitted to the court and the prosecutor's office, registration, and other documents necessary for application for registration. A Certified Judicial Scrivener also bears the duty of care of a good manager in performing these duties. Individually, they have the duty to notify the best business process and business process for the client. In addition, they have the duty to explain and advise the client. For example, if a Certified Judicial Scrivener entrusted with real estate registration does not explain to the client that a secured right cannot be established on the real estate, he or she is liable for damages resulting from the breach of the duty of explanation.[81] In addition, the Certified Judicial Scrivener is obliged to verify the person responsible for the registration work so that wrong registration does not occur. If there is any circumstance to suspect that the person is the proper person in charge of it, the identity of the person should be checked through various methods. Therefore, if property damage occurs to a third party due to his or her negligence, the Certified Judicial Scrivener is liable for the damage. Article 26(1) of the Certified Judicial Scrivener Act stipulates that a Certified Judicial Scrivener shall be responsible for compensation for damage to the property of a delegator caused by him or her by intent or negligence in performing his or her duties. For a third party who is not a mandator, the Certified Judicial Scrivener bears the liability for damages in accordance with Article 750 of the Korean Civil Code.

IV. Builders and Architects

81. A contractor who has received a construction work contract from a building owner bears the liability for Warranty. Thus, the contractor is liable for the damage to the owner for defects in the building and bears the tort liability to a third party who has suffered damage due to defects in the building. In addition to the Korean Civil Code, Article 44(1) of the "Framework Act on the Construction Industry" stipulates that if a constructor inflicts any damage to any third person by unconscientiously performing construction works, by intention or negligence, he or she is

79. Supreme Court Decision 93Da62508, decided May 12, 1995.
80. Supreme Court Decision 90DaKa27396, decided Dec. 7, 1990.
81. Supreme Court Decision 2010Da5892, decided Sep. 29, 2011.

liable for the damage. However, if the contractor's tort liability against a third party is recognized, the owner, the client, is liable for tortious acts against the third party "when the contractor is at gross negligence with respect to the contract or instructions" pursuant to Article 757 of the Korean Civil Code.

In South Korea, due to high population density and urbanization, there are many complex buildings such as apartments. For this reason, some special laws (Acts on Ownership and Management of Collective Buildings, etc.) have been enacted regarding the types of defects and the period of warranty liability for defects in collective buildings. In the case of Korea, due to the high population density and urbanization, there are many buildings such as apartments. Therefore, with respect to defects in collective buildings, some special laws regarding the type of defects and the period of liability for defects (Act on Ownership and Management of Condominium Buildings) have been enacted. The civil liability of the contractor to a third party has often been problematic in cases where the occupants of a neighboring building are held liable for tort because the sunlight and views of the occupants of the neighboring buildings have been infringed upon during the construction of the building. The South Korean Supreme Court held "the contractor of a building construction project constructs the building by fulfilling the obligations stipulated in the contract, so it is a principle. Therefore, it would be said that there is no liability for damages for the obstruction of sunlight. However, when the contractor constructs a building for the purpose of obstructing the sunshine enjoyed by others by himself or herself or with the contractor. He knew or could have known that the building construction was in violation of related building statutes and that it would interfere with the sunlight enjoyed by others. Nevertheless, if there is a special circumstance, such as when the building is built without knowing this by negligence, or when the building is built with a shared interest as a de facto joint project entity with the contractor, the contractor is also liable for damages for obstruction of sunlight."[82]

82. Only architects can design and supervise buildings as stipulated by law (Article 4 of the Certified Architects Act). Considering the significant impact of building quality and safety management on society in general, a professional with certain qualifications is in charge of designing and supervising buildings. Architects are obligated to prepare design drawings in accordance with the building design contract with the client. In this case, the architect must comply with the standards of relevant laws, such as the standards for drafting design documents. In addition, architects are responsible for explaining and giving advice to the client regarding the overall construction as an architectural expert. If there is negligence concerning the design, the architect is responsible for the breach of contract to the owner, and if a third party suffers damage, he or she also bears the tort liability. If the breach of obligation concerning the design overlaps with the breach of duty under the contract for construction, both liabilities are in a relationship of jointly and severally liable to make compensation for such damages.[83]

---

82. Supreme Court Decision 2004Da38792, decided Mar. 24, 2005.
83. Supreme Court Decision 2012Da89320, decided Feb. 26, 2015.

Supervision refers to the act of a person designated as a construction supervisor, under his or her own responsibility, to check whether a building is being constructed according to the contents of the design document, as stipulated by the Building Act, and to guide and supervise construction management and safety management.

The supervisor is also liable for tortious acts against a third party other than the owner due to the negligence of the supervisory duty. There are not many judgments regarding the civil liability of architects due to negligence in design. However, civil liability for a supervisor's poor supervision is recognized in the following cases. For example, if the design drawings and other construction work are neglected because the site has not been properly checked[84] or there is a failure to exercise due care to ensure that instructions to the builder have been properly completed.[85] In the case of a defect in the building caused by not finding any design errors.

V. Others (CPA, Certified Appraiser)

83. In South Korea, a professional, such as a certified tax accountant,[86] a bank,[87] or a licensed real estate agent,[88] who has professional knowledge and ability and enjoys social trust in his or her professional activities, such as his written opinion, is liable for economic damage as tort liability to a third party other than the contracting party for his or her work negligence. Civil liability for negligence in notary service may also fall within the domain of professional responsibility. However, in South Korea, a notary public performs the notary duties in the status of a quasi-public official. Therefore, the state is liable for damages in accordance with the State Compensation Act for damages resulting from poor notary service. In addition, the notary is directly liable to individual victims for the tort in case of intentional or gross negligence. Here, we introduce the civil liability of CPAs and certified appraisers to third parties.

84. Certified Public Accountant.

A certified public accountant, as an expert in accounting, shall perform his or her duties fairly and diligently, such as auditing, appraisal, and tax representation related to accounting. In addition, certified public accountants must maintain independence in the performance of their duties and must not intentionally hide the truth or make false reports (Articles 2 and 15 of the CPA Act). The accounting audit task of a certified public accountant is to audit the financial statements for the purpose of displaying and reporting the financial condition and management performance of a company to a third party. Therefore, the result has a significant impact on third parties who have trusted and invested in it other than the mandator.

84. Supreme Court Decision 86Daka23789320, decided Mar. 14, 1989.
85. Supreme Court Decision 99Da70365, decided Sep. 7, 2001.
86. Supreme Court Decision 2011Da87655, decided Sep. 12, 2013 (Liability for damages resulting from free and incorrect tax consultation).
87. Supreme Court Decision 2006Da20405, decided Jul. 26, 2007.
88. Supreme Court Decision 91Da36239, decided Feb. 11, 1992 (Duty to investigate and confirm whether the person who intends to sell is the real right holder).

Korean case law has recognized the tort liability of Article 750 of the Korean Civil Code to a certified public accountant for economic damage suffered by a third party as a result of such a credible position of a certified public accountant. In addition to the Korean Civil Code, Article 31(2) of the "Act on External Audit of Stock Companies" provides that if an auditor who has failed to enter important matters or has made a false statement on an audit report and thereby causes damage to a third party who has relied on and used such report, the auditor is liable for damages to the third party. According to Korean precedents and the majority theory of South Korean scholars, both liabilities are in a relationship of contention for claims. Therefore, an investment victim who suffered losses due to poor auditing can ask the certified public account for both liabilities.[89]

85. Certified Appraiser.

A certified appraise does the job of appraising land and its fixtures at the request of clients. The result of the appraisal has a significant influence on the price determination in the transaction of the appraisal object. Therefore, appraisers with nationally accredited qualifications are required to perform the work. A certified appraiser shall conduct an appraisal fairly and in good faith.

Where an appraisal corporation, etc., causes harm to an appraisal requester or a third party in good faith by conducting an appraisal, the outcome of which shows a marked difference from fair value at the time of appraisal by intention or mistake, or by recording deceit in the appraisal report, the appraisal corporation, etc., shall be liable for damages (Article 28(1) of Act on Appraisal and Certified Appraisers). In this provision, "third party in good faith" refers to the one who does not recognize that the appraisal content is false or that there is a significant difference from the fair price at the time of appraisal. In addition, if the appraisal report states that the appraisal report cannot be used for other than the purpose of requesting an appraisal, or that no one other than the appraisal client can use it, it means a person who is unaware of the fact that such appraisal has been used.[90]

§2. Liability of Public Authorities

86. Article 29(1) of the South Korean Constitution stipulates that in case a person has sustained damages by an unlawful act committed by a public official in the course of official duties, he or she may claim just compensation from the State or public organization under the conditions as prescribed by Act. Therefore, the liability of the state or public organizations is generally recognized. The South Korean constitution renounces the sovereign immunity of the state, which is the subject of public power, and recognizes the responsibility for compensation. To specifically implement this, the State Compensation Act has been enacted. The State Compensation Act explicitly recognizes the liability of the state or local governments for

89. Supreme Court Decision 97Da26555, decided Oct. 22, 1999; Supreme Court Decision 97Da32215, decided Apr. 24, 1998.

90. Supreme Court Decision 99Da28661, decided Sep. 7, 1999; Supreme Court Decision 2006Da64627, decided Sep. 10, 2009.

damages caused by illegal acts of public officials and damage caused by defects in the installation and management of public structures.[91] There is a theory that understands the nature of the State Compensation Act as a public law. However, the majority of South Korean scholars understand the State Compensation Act as a private law and as a special law to the Korean Civil Code. Courts also have treated the case for claiming State compensation as a normal civil litigation case.

87. Article 2(1) of the State Compensation Act stipulates that where public officials inflict damage on other persons by intention or negligence in performing their official duties in violation of the statutes, the State or local governments shall compensate for such damage. According to this, the liability requirements of the State Compensation Act are: (1) public officials (including private persons entrusted with public duties), (2) while performing their duties, (3) intentionally or negligently, (4) violating statutes, and (5) inflicting damage to others. First, the term "public official" includes those who are entrusted with public service and are actually engaged in public service other than those who have the status of a public official. For example, civilians in transportation work entrusted with public duties[92] such as child protection and transportation guidance from local governments, and employees of private enterprises entrusted with storage of seized property by prosecutors. Public officials with frequent problems with the application of the State Compensation Act include police officers, correctional officers, tax officials, teachers of national and public schools, public officials in charge of registration or seal, and execution officers. Second, the relevance of the unlawful act to the performance of duties must be recognized. The performance of duties means not only administrative but also legislative and judicial functions. The scope includes not only the authority action under the public law but also the management action under the public law. However, the private and economic actions of the state or local governments are not subject to the State Compensation Act. Third, the act must be the intention or negligence of a public official. In order to cope with the increased risk due to the complexity and specialization of administrative activities, the requirement for intention and negligence objectively and formally grasps the concept of negligence. The South Korean Supreme Court held "when any administrative disposition is later canceled, it is difficult to conclude that the administrative disposition constitutes a tortious act due to the intention or negligence of a public official. However, when it is recognized that the administrative disposition has lost its objective justification due to the lack of objective due diligence, when the public official in charge of the administrative disposition is regarded as a standard public official, the requirement for state liability under Article 2 of the State Compensation Act is satisfied." At this time, whether objective legitimacy has been lost is determined by taking into account various circumstances such as the mode and purpose of the

91. The Constitution stipulates that the person responsible is "the state or a public organization." On the other hand, the State Compensation Act defines as "the State or local government." Therefore, public organizations other than local governments are liable for compensation in accordance with the Korean Civil Code, not the State Compensation Act.
92. Supreme Court Decision 98Da39060, decided Jan. 5, 2001.

administrative disposition that constitutes an infringing act, whether or not the victim is involved and the degree of involvement, the type of infringed profit and the degree of damage. In addition, it is judged that the judgment should be made by examining the practical reasons for making the state or local governments bear the responsibility for compensating for damages.[93] As for the burden of proof regarding the intention or negligence of a public official, it is widely argued that if the victim proves that public authority was illegally exercised by the public official, the intention or negligence of the public official is in fact presumed. However, according to the traditional view that state liability for compensation is a type of civil liability, the burden of proving the intentional or negligence of a public official is borne by the victim.[94] Fourth, there must be an act of violating statutes by public officials. This includes not only laws in the strict sense but also the principle of good faith and good public order. It also includes cases where the performance of public duties act loses its objective legitimacy. Even in the case of administrative rules, legality is not recognized. However, in view of the fact that administrative rules are objective standards for administrative actions, if unfavorable dispositions are taken in violation of administrative rules without reasonable grounds, it is a "violation of statutes" in Article 2 of the State Compensation Act.

However, if the purpose of protection of statutes in which public officials violated their duties is not to protect the interests and safety of individual members of society but merely to regulate internal order in administrative agencies (lack of third-party relevance of relevant laws and regulations), liability for damages according to the State Compensation Act may not be recognized.[95]

Acts of violation of statutes by public officials are not limited to active actions but can also be satisfied by omissions if the duty to act is recognized. However, in case of omission, it is left to the discretion of the public official whether to exercise the executive power. Therefore, it cannot be immediately determined that it is illegal because a public official does not exercise his or her authority. "How serious and imminent the legal interests of the people or the damage caused to the people are infringed due to the negligence of public officials, and whether there is a possibility that the relevant public officials can anticipate such consequences and take measures to avoid the consequences are taken into account" to determine the illegality.[96] In addition, with respect to the liability for compensation due to the duties of special public officials engaged in legislative affairs, such as members of the National Assembly, or judicial affairs, such as judges and prosecutors, in light of the characteristics of their duties, the recognition of illegality is considered higher and stricter than in the case of general public officials.[97]

---

93. Supreme Court Decision 2008Da30703, decided Jan. 27, 2011.
94. Seo, Ki-Seok, *The Commentary of Korean Civil Code—Law of Obligations (7)*, State Compensation Act, 81.
95. South Korean courts held that illegality is not recognized in such cases. Also, South Korean courts determined that when it has been judged that the significant causal relationship necessary to establish responsibility between the breach of duty and damage of public officials is not recognized.
96. Supreme Court Decision 98Da18520, decided Oct. 13, 1998.
97. Supreme Court Decision 96Da56115, decided Jun. 13, 1997; Supreme Court Decision 2000Da16114, decided Apr. 24, 2001.

88. If the national or local government is recognized for liability under the State Compensation Act, the individual responsibility of public officials becomes an issue. According to Article 2(2) of the State Compensation Act, the State or local government that compensates the victim for damage may indemnify the public official if the public official is intentionally or grossly negligent.

There are conflicting views as to whether a victim can directly claim compensation for damages from an individual public official.[98] According to the Korean Supreme Court ruling, if a public official inflicts damage on others through an illegal act while performing his or her duties, the state shall bear the responsibility for compensation. However, it is construed that the individual public official shall not be liable for damages if the public official is only at light fault.[99] The purpose of exempting civil servants from personal responsibility for light negligence is to secure the safety of public officials in the execution of their official duties. Even in this case, the legal status of the victim is not unreasonably limited because the liability for compensation by the state with sufficient compensatory power is recognized.

89. Article 5(1) of the State Compensation Act stipulates that when damage is caused to another person due to a defect in the installation or management of roads, rivers, or other public buildings, the State or local government shall compensate for the damage. This provision is understood as the state liability for compensation corresponding to Article 758 of the Korean Civil Code on Civil Liability of Individuals due to Defects in Installation and Preservation of Structures. According to Article 5(1) of the State Compensation Act, in the case of damage caused by defects in the installation and management of the spiritual building, the defense by the state or local governments that they were not negligent in preventing the damage is excluded. However, if the defect of the structure is caused by the act of a third party or force majeure such as a natural disaster, or accessing or using the structure while recognizing the danger (such as pollution, including noise), the liability of the state or local governments is excluded.

90. According to the State Compensation Act, the Compensation Council is established and operated to deliberate on cases of claims for damages against the state or local governments. Upon receipt of an application for compensation, the compensation council shall decide whether to pay compensation within a certain period of time. Victims who are dissatisfied with this may apply for a retrial to the Superior Compensation Council. In the past, a claim for compensation through an administrative procedure must have been filed before filing a claim for compensation with the court. (prepositionalism of compensation decision). However, since the revision of the State Compensation Act in 2000, victims can immediately file a claim for compensation in court without filing a claim for compensation with the compensation council.

98. *See* Kim, Yu-jin, *The Commentary of Korean Civil Code—Law of Obligations (7)*, 243–245, 2022.
99. Supreme Court en banc Decision 95Da38677 Decided Feb. 15, 1996.

§3. Abuse of Rights

91. In principle, the actions of the parties involved in the litigation are legal in order to ensure the use of the judicial system for the realization and protection of rights and not to unreasonably restrict it. Accordingly, litigation-related acts can only be tortious acts in special cases: they can be divided into an act of filing a lawsuit and an act of unfair enforcement.

92. The Supreme Court of South Korea decided as to whether an unfair lawsuit is a tortious act as follows. "If the person who initiated the civil action lost his or her case, the fact that such a lawsuit is a tortious act against the other party means that the right or legal relationship asserted by the complainant in the lawsuit has no factual or legal basis. It is limited to cases in which the person who filed the lawsuit is aware of such facts or the lawsuit is filed despite the fact that ordinary people can easily understand it.[100] In recognizing the illegality and fault of the unfair lawsuit, the following factors were taken into account: the motive or purpose of filing the lawsuit and whether the complainant knew or did not know that his right did not exist, even though he could have easily known this, he did not even conduct a minimum legal and factual investigation. In the case of answering a legal suit or appeal, it is judged as in the case of litigation. Thus, "in the guise of the realization of rights or protection of rights, infringing on the rights or interests of the other party, or causing suffering to the other party without any reasonable reason. Therefore, when intention or negligent is recognized and it is against public order, the illegality is recognized and constitutes a tortious act."[101] Similarly, in the case of accusations and charges that seek punishment for criminals, it determines whether the act is tortious.[102]

93. In the case where compulsory execution causes damage to a third party due to violation of laws and regulations on enforcement procedures, in principle, the liability of the state and enforcement agencies for damages will be an issue. However, if, for example, the creditor does not suspend the execution of the execution officer without delay or does not apply for recission even though the creditor knows that it is the property of a third person, thereby causing damage to a third party, the liability of the creditor who initiated the execution procedure is problematic.

In addition, although the execution creditor made the execution without knowing that it was the property of a third party, the tort liability may be recognized if the execution status was maintained when the execution object was later known or could have been easily known as the possession of the third party.[103] In addition, the tort liability is recognized in the case where a party commits to deceive the other party or the court, obtains a final judgment on a claim that does not exist in substance, and causes damage to the other party's property by forcibly executing it.

100. Supreme Court Decision 2010Da15363 Decided Jul. 10, 2010.
101. Supreme Court Decision 2005Da31033 Decided Apr. 26, 2007 (answering a legal suit).
102. Supreme Court Decision 95Da321211 Decided Sep. 5, 1997.
103. Supreme Court Decision 98Da59767 Decided Apr. 9, 1999.

However, this would result in denial of the subjugation of the final judgment. Therefore, it is limited to cases where the execution based on the final judgment is remarkably unfair and it is clear that it is against justice to have the other party accept the execution. For example, if a party to the litigation interferes with the other party's involvement in the litigation with the intent to injure the other party's rights or deceive the court with false allegations, the judgment is made in a state where there are grounds for reexamination of the final judgment or other party's fundamental procedural rights are seriously violated. In these cases, the liability for tort by compulsory execution has been acknowledged.[104]

Lastly, with respect to defamation by pleading, there may be cases in which the reputation of others may be damaged by the pleadings of the parties or lawyers or the testimony of witnesses in civil litigation or criminal litigation. However, defamation is inevitable in the process of litigation, such as pleading, in that litigation is a forum for offensive methods between opposing parties. Thus, it cannot be treated in the same way as in the case of general defamation. Therefore, defamation by pleadings, etc., is not illegal in principle, and it can be judged exceptionally illegal only when it is clear that it is outside the socially permitted range.

§4. Injury to Reputation and Privacy

94. Liability for damages due to infringement of honor or privacy is recognized under the general provisions of Article 750 of the Korean Civil Code on the grounds of infringement of personal rights. The Korean Civil Code has only a provision on defamation, but the rights of personality, such as protection of privacy and the right to name and portrait, have greatly developed according to the development of precedents and theories in the 1970s and 1980s.

95. Defamation is an act that infringes on a person's social evaluation, such as character, virtue, reputation, and credibility. Judgment of the illegality of defamation for civil liability is conducted based on the grounds for exclusion of the illegality of defamation under Article 310 of the Korean Criminal Code. Article 310 of the Criminal Act stipulates that "If a person who defames another by publicly alleging facts are true and solely for the public interest, the act is not punishable." In a case in which liability for defamation caused by media organizations by bringing out the signs of "public interest" and "authenticity (or relevancy)," the South Korean Supreme Court held as follows. "Although an act defames others, if it is in the public interest, and thus the purpose is solely for the public good, and if there is proof that it is true, there is no illegality in this act. Also, in the absence of such proof, there is no illegality if the agent has good reason to believe it to be true."[105] Whether the content of the report is for the public interest, "all circumstances should be taken into account, such as regarding the expression itself, the specific content of the facts in a timely manner, the scope of the other party to whom the facts were

104. Supreme Court Decision 4292Minsang656 Decided Nov. 3, 1960; Supreme Court Decision 84Daka572 Decided Jul. 24, 1984; Supreme Court Decision 99Da32899 Decided Nov. 13, 2001.
105. Supreme Court Decision 85Daka29 Decided Oct. 11, 1988.

published, and the method of expression. At the same time, a decision shall be made by comparing and considering the degree of damage to the reputation that may be damaged by the expression. If the main purpose or motive of the actor is for the public interest, it should be viewed as for the public interest even if other private motives are included."[106] If the news content has a public interest, there is no illegality if the news content is true or if there is reason to believe that it is true even if it is not true. Whether or not it is relevant is determined by comprehensively considering various circumstances, such as whether prompt reporting is requested due to the nature of the article, whether the source is reliable, and whether it is easy to confirm the truth, by face-to-face meetings with the victim.[107] In the case of defamation of public figures such as politicians and high-ranking public officials, South Korea was also influenced by American judgment principles. Therefore, in order to actively protect the freedom of expression for monitoring and criticizing public activities, the illegality of the report is acknowledged if it is malicious or an attack that has significantly lost its relevance.[108] Furthermore, in civil defamation acts, tortious acts can be established not only by expressing facts but also by expressing opinions or comments. In this case, the illegality is not based on whether the opinion or comment itself is true or objectively just. However, the illegality test is based on whether there is evidence that the facts underlying the opinion or comment are true in important respects. Or if there is no such proof, it is judged according to whether the person who made the act of expression has good reason to believe that the facts premised on it are true in substantial respects.[109] With respect to the burden of proof regarding the illegality of defamation, the plaintiff must prove the falsehood of the stated facts, and the defendant must prove the grounds for exclusion of illegality.[110]

96. Regarding tort liability under Article 750 of the Korean Civil Code on the grounds of invasion of privacy, in a case in which the victim's identity was exposed in the process of broadcasting the side effects of plastic surgery, the Supreme Court of Korea ruled as follows. "People have a legal interest in not disclosing the secrets of their private life to others without permission. Accordingly, matters concerning the confidentiality of an individual's private life should be protected as secrets, unless they relate to the public interest and are of legitimate interest to the public. Unduly disclosing this constitutes a tortious act. It is not illegal to disclose matters related to a person's private life within the scope of the consent after obtaining his or her consent. However, even if the person's consent is obtained, it is illegal to disclose such matters for a purpose or method different from that expected at the time of consent, exceeding the scope of consent."[111] Also, in the case of public figures, the South Korean Supreme Court said, "the privacy and freedom of private life are restricted within a certain range, and the disclosure of the private life may be exempted. However, in the case of public figures, they are subject to the public's

106. Supreme Court Decision 95Daka36329 Decided Dec. 11, 1996.
107. Supreme Court Decision 97Da24207 Decided Sep. 30, 1997.
108. Supreme Court Decision 20007Da14613 Decided Dec. 24, 2002.
109. Supreme Court Decision 98Da31356 Decided Feb. 9, 1999.
110. Supreme Court Decision 2005Da58823 Decided Jan. 24, 2008.
111. Supreme Court Decision 96Da11327 Decided Sep. 4, 1998.

right to know, and their disclosure is in the public interest. Therefore, regardless of the public's right to know, if a state agency secretly collects personal information for the purpose of monitoring daily trends, it cannot be exempted just because the subject is a public person."

97. In relation to the infringement of the personality right of a corporation, the personality right recognized by a natural person cannot be recognized as it is by a corporation. For example, personal legal interests such as life, body, health, and privacy are not recognized as a corporation. However, even in the case of a corporation, protection against damage to reputation and trust must be recognized in light of the corporation's social activities. South Korean Supreme Court also held that if the social reputation and credibility of a corporation are infringed, and the social evaluation of the corporation is infringed, it constitutes a tortious act against the corporation.[112] However, in the case of violations of personality rights, such as defamation of the deceased, it is necessary to protect the personality rights even after the death of the person. However, there is a difficulty in protecting the personality rights of the deceased in that a person has rights and abilities while he is alive (Article 3 of the Korean Civil Code). There is an opposing view that attempts to constitute a violation of the personality right to the deceased and one that attempts to constitute a violation of the personality right to the bereaved family. In a lower court judgment in South Korea, it has been recognized as an infringement of the personality right of the deceased.[113]

98. Civil remedies for protecting personality rights include the right to claim damages, appropriate measures to restore reputation in case of defamation, and the right to request an injunction. In addition, in the case of infringement of personality rights by the press, the "Act on Press Arbitration and Remedies for Damage Caused by Press Reports" stipulates (1) the right to require the relevant press organization to report on a corrected statement, (2) the right to require the relevant press organization to report on a contradictory statement, and (3) right to require the relevant press organization to make further reports.

The general remedy for infringement of personality rights is the right to claim damages for tortious acts. Compensation for damages is the payment of non-economic damage, which is compensation for mental damage. In the payment of non-economic damage, the court considers the motive of the infringement, the intention or negligence of the tortfeasor, and the social status and occupation of both parties. For example, in the case of the slander advertisement, the South Korean Supreme Court held that "The Court considers the type and nature of the damage suffered by the plaintiff, the plaintiff's reputation and business credibility, the size and business performance of the plaintiff's company, the degree of falsehood and the intensity of the slander in the advertisements in this case, and the defendant's advertising behavior. In addition, the Court takes into account of the degree of maliciousness revealed in general, the immediacy and continuity of the effects of negative advertisements, the difficulty of recovering from the negative effects, the size

112. Supreme Court Decision 93Da40614, 40621 Decided Apr. 12, 1996.
113. Seoul District Court Decision 94Kahap9230, Jun. 23, 1995.

and wealth of the defendant company."[114] Also, the right to request for injunction is recognized for the infringement of personality rights.

The right to request an injunction for infringement of personality rights is not explicitly stipulated. However, the South Korean Supreme Court held, "Due to the nature of the personality right, it is difficult to completely recover the damage only with remedies (such as monetary compensation or disposition for restoration of reputation) after it has been violated. Also, it is difficult to expect the effectiveness of compensation for damages. Accordingly, the right to request injunction, such as suspension or prevention of infringement, is also recognized as a preemptive (preventive) remedy for infringement of personality rights."[115] However, even recognizing the right to request injunction, especially the right to request injunction on media reports, may be a restriction on the freedom of expression protected by the Constitution. Therefore, it must be recognized under strict conditions compared to compensation for damages, which is an *ex post* remedy. The Korean Supreme Court also ruled as follows. "If the content of the expression is not true or it is in the public interest, its purpose is not solely for the public interest. Thus, when there is a risk of inflicting significant and remarkably irreparable damage to the victim, it is clear that such an act of expression is not superior to the victim's honor. In addition, the necessity of injunction is recognized as an effective and appropriate remedy for it. Therefore, the preemptive injunction is permitted only when these substantive requirements are satisfied."[116]

Article 764 of the Korean Civil Code provides that the court may, on the application of the injured party, order the person who has defamed another's reputation to take measures appropriate for repairing the injured party's reputation, either in lieu of or together with provision of compensation. Appropriate dispositions for the restoration of reputation include a request for a corrected statement, and a request for withdrawal and cancelation. In the past, apology advertisements were considered appropriate measures to restore reputation, but in 1991, the South Korean Constitutional Court decided that apology advertisements violated the Constitution.[117]

§5. Interference by a Third Person with Contractual Relations

99. Infringement of contractual interests, such as infringement of claims, which are relative rights based on a contract, infringement of another's contractual relationship, or inducement of wrong conclusion of a contract, is also considered a tortious act in South Korea with the general provisions of Article 750 of the Korean Civil Code. It is the cause of liability for damages caused by a tortious act. Unlike real rights, claims, which are relative rights, are often not disclosed to a third party. Also, the infringement of claims itself may be justified on the basis of the principle of free competition. Accordingly, it is not always illegal for a third party to infringe

114. Supreme Court Decision 93Da40614, 40621 Decided Apr. 12, 1996.
115. Supreme Court Decision 93Da40614, 40621 Decided Apr. 12, 1996.
116. Supreme Court Decision 2003Ma1477, Decided Jan. 17, 2005.
117. Constitutional Court Decision 89Hunma160, Decided Apr. 1, 1991.

upon a claim. However, a tortious act can be constituted only in certain cases in consideration of the form of the infringing act.

The South Korean Supreme Court is consistent with the following rule. "Infringement of claims by a third party may constitute tort. However, third party infringement is not always a tortious act. Depending on the form of claim infringement, it shall be determined in detail by examining whether it is a tortious act or not. In a competitive contractual relationship between independent economic entities, with just the fact that a third party simply enters into a contract that violates the contract between the debtor and the creditor while knowing the details of the contract between the debtor and the creditor, it is not enough to admit the third party's intention, or negligence and illegality. Therefore, only in cases where there are special circumstances, such as that a third party actively colluded with the debtor, or that the third party used means contrary to social norms such as deception or intimidation or concluded a contract with the debtor with the intention of harming the creditor, the third party' intention, negligence and illegality is acknowledged."[118]

100. When tort liability becomes a problem for the reason of infringement of contractual legal interests, the following are the cases. The share transferor has violated the obligation to have the first transferee acquire full rights to the transferred shares. The share transferor has already disposed of and transferred the shares that do not belong to him to a third party. The stock transferor has the second transferee acquire the full rights by receiving the transfer of title in the register of shareholders. As a result, the first transferee could not exercise the rights of the shareholder. In this case, the South Korean Supreme Court recognized the tort liability of the transferor.[119] In addition, when an employee or executive retires from his or her company and uses the technical or managerial information of the former company to engage in unfair competition activities to take over the customer of the former company. Or, if a competitor unfairly induces or hires other business operators to interfere with the business activities of other business operators, it also constitutes tort liability on the ground of infringing on the contractual relationship of others.[120] Furthermore, the South Korean Supreme Court recognized tortious actions in these cases: (1) the union interferes with the business activities of the company by engaging in an unjustified industrial action,[121] (2) a civic group illegally terminates the contract by threatening to boycott a performance partner that has signed a ticket sales contract with the performance agency as part of opposing the performance of a specific singer for the public interest.[122]

Recently, the tort liability was also recognized for acts that led to the conclusion of a contract that was economically disadvantageous according to wrongful acts prior to the establishment of the contract. For example, if a person engaged in insurance solicitation for an insurance company causes damage to a customer by failing

118. Supreme Court Decision 99Da38699, Decided May 8, 2001.
119. Supreme Court Decision 2012Da38780, Decided Nov. 29, 2012.
120. However, in the above case, special laws such as the Unfair Competition Prevention and Trade Secret Protection Act, Monopoly Regulation and Fair Trade Act stipulate liability for damages due to unfair competition activities.
121. Supreme Court Decision 93Da32828, 32835, Decided Mar. 35, 1994.
122. Supreme Court Decision 98Da51091, Decided Jun. 13, 2001.

to properly explain to the customer important matters of the insurance contract, such as the payment of premiums, the reason for the payment of insurance money, and the characteristics and risks of insurance products, the person is liable for the damage caused by tortious acts pursuant to the Article 750 of the Korean Civil Code.[123] In addition, in the process of selling real estate, such as apartments and shopping malls, false or exaggerated advertisements are made against the facts regarding the construction of a landfill site near the building for sale and the installation plan of a densely populated facility. In this case, the civil tort liability is recognized for the violation of the duty to explain in good faith.[124]

Civil liability to third parties due to negligent performances of professionals such as real estate agents and the civil liability of financial investment companies for violating their duty to explain to prospective investors have been increasing.

§6. OTHERS

101. Liability for torts has constantly reflected the changes and developments of the times in South Korea. In the 1990s and 2000s, as individualization and democratization of Korean society progressed, conflicts between the fundamental rights protected by the constitution became issues. Liability for torts also plays a role in guaranteeing fundamental rights in such conflict situations. For example, the South Korean Supreme Court decided on the following issues: (1) religious education in private schools when the freedom of religious education in private schools established by religious organizations conflict with the freedom of students to engage in passive religious practices.[125] (2) rationality and limit of the discrimination of members based on gender based on the principle of private autonomy (or freedom of association) of private organizations.[126] (3) when an employer pays lower wages to female workers than male workers without reasonable reasons even though the labor provided by male and female workers working within the same business is of the same value, it constitutes a tortious act.[127]

However, tort liability also performs a public function to establish a fair transaction order by protecting substantial contractual freedom. These cases are obligation of the bank to explain the terms and conditions of loan products to bank users;[128] the insurance company's obligation to explain the insurance products;[129] the obligation of a financial investment company to comply with the principle of suitability in recommending investment in financial products and to explain the products and risks to be invested to customers;[130] the issuer's liability for damages in accordance with false or inaccurate statements in the securities declaration form

123. Supreme Court Decision 2012Da22242, Decided Oct. 27, 2014.
124. Supreme Court Decision 2004Da48515, Decided Oct. 12, 2006.
125. Supreme Court en banc Decision 2008Da38288 Decided Apr. 22, 2010.
126. Supreme Court Decision 2009Da19864 Decided Jan. 27, 2011.
127. Supreme Court Decision 2012Da31734 Decided Jan.16, 2013.
128. Supreme Court Decision 2000Da30943 Decided Apr. 27, 2001.
129. Supreme Court Decision 2010Da34159 Decided Jun. 13, 2013.
130. Supreme Court Decision 2000Da30943 Decided Apr. 27, 2001.

and investment prospectus necessary for the public offering of securities;[131] external auditor's liability for negligence of accounting fraud.[132] In addition, in recent years, the tort liability due to the risk of damage caused by the development of the Internet and science and technology has also been increasing. According to South Korea's high-speed Internet usage rate, responsibility for illegal collection and provision of personal information through the Internet and illegal leakage have been frequent problems.[133] Furthermore, stem cell transplantation, according to the development of genetic engineering, has been performed for therapeutic purposes. Accordingly, the doctor's duty to explain medical practices in the clinical trial stage[134] and liability for damages due to defects in products produced by intensive technology have also been dealt with.[135]

131. Supreme Court Decision 99Da48979 Decided May 14, 2002.
132. Supreme Court Decision 2007Da90647 Decided Jun. 26, 2008.
133. Supreme Court Decision 2014Da235080 Decided Aug. 17, 2016; Supreme Court Decision 2013Da43994, 44003 Decided Feb. 12, 2015.
134. Supreme Court Decision 2007Da3162 Decided Oct. 14, 2010.
135. Supreme Court Decision 2003Da16771 Decided Mar. 12, 2004 (sudden acceleration incident on an automobile).

Part II. Liability for Acts of Others

Chapter 1. Vicarious Liability

§1. Employee/Employer

102. The employer's liability for compensation for an employee's tortious acts is regulated in Article 756 of the Korean Civil Code. Article 756(1) of the Korean Civil Code provides that a person who employs another to perform a specific affair is liable for compensating for any loss inflicted on a third person by the employee in the course of performing the specific affair, provided that this shall not apply where the employer has exercised due care in appointing the employee, and in supervising the performance of the specific affair, or where the loss has been inflicted even if the employer has exercised due care. Regarding the nature of liability under Article 756(1) of the Korean Civil Code, there are two opinions: one is a subrogation responsibility and the other is an inherent responsibility due to the employer's own negligence. According to the position of subrogation responsibility, the purpose of employer responsibility is to guarantee the victim's right to claim compensation for the employee. Accordingly, the employer's liability for compensation arises only when the employee's tort liability is recognized. However, according to the position of self-responsibility theory (as stipulated in the proviso to Article 756(1) of the Korean Civil Code), the basis of the employer's responsibility lies in the employer's own fault for not properly appointing or supervising the employee. This position is the dominant view in South Korea.

103. The grounds for employer responsibility pursuant to Article 756(1) of the Korean Civil Code are: (1) an employee's infringement, (2) the existence of an employer-employee relationship, (3) the relevance of business of employer, and (4) the employer's negligence in the appointment and supervision of the employee. First, the employee must have committed an illegal act against a third party. At this time, the question is whether the employee's illegal act must satisfy the tort requirement of Article 750 of the Korean Civil Code. The Korean Supreme Court has held that the employer's liability for compensation is only recognized when the employee's intention/negligence and tort responsibility are established and the employee's tortious liability to the victim is recognized.[136]

---

136. In this regard, South Korean scholars supporting the theory of self-responsibility explain that the employee's negligence and tort responsibility do not matter to the employer's liability to 3rd parties. Therefore, they criticize the position of the case law.

104. As the second requirement of employer responsibility, there must be a relationship between the employer and the employee. The core of the relationship is that the employee must be in a subordinate relationship under the direction and supervision of the employer. The employment relationship is a broader concept than the employment or labor contract relationship, and it is also recognized in title lending and partnerships. The South Korean Supreme Court held that regardless of whether the employer actually commanded or supervised, the decision should be made based on whether the employer was in a position to direct and supervise the tortfeasor from an objective and normative perspective.[137] For example, a person who permits another person to conduct business using his or her name may bear the employer's liability under Article 756 of the Korean Civil Code for the tortious act to a third party.[138] Even in the partnership relationship, if the relationship of command and supervision with respect to the execution of business is recognized, the business partner may be both in the positions of a business partner and of an employer.[139]

In addition, the employment relationship is not limited to a valid employment relationship. It is sufficient for a person to temporarily execute business affairs under the scope of his or her command and supervision for another.[140] The cause of the employer-employee relationship, the presence or absence of wages, or the length or length of the relationship period do not matter. Moreover, the South Korean Supreme Court held that even in the case of mandate (unlike many theories of Korean scholars), there is a command and supervisory relationship between the mandator and the mandatory. Thus, in a case in which an attorney who took charge of the division of inherited property sold the real estate to another person and obtained the money for the property, the employer's responsibility of mandator is recognized.[141]

105. In order for the employer's liability to be recognized, the employee's infringement to a third party must be related to the employer's business performance. According to the theory of appearance, majority view of Korean scholars and the Supreme Court have recognized the relevance of business performance when the employee's acts have the appearance of business performance. In other words, when an employee's act that causes damage is objectively related to the employer's business activity or performance (without considering the employee's subjective intention), it is regarded as an activity related to business performance. For example, the South Supreme Court recognizes business relevance in the following cases: (1) an employee who was in charge of collecting and organizing scrap papers and scrap metals for the company's production site cleaning gave a pesticide as a drink to the victim who came to collect the scrap metal, and the victim drank it and died.[142] (2) a bank's loan officer deceives the borrower into receiving a portion of the loan for future interest payments.[143] The appearance theory broadly

137. Supreme Court Decision 2003Da36133 Decided Feb. 25, 2005.
138. Supreme Court Decision 94Da24176 Decided Oct. 25, 1994.
139. Supreme Court Decision 2005Da65562 Decided Mar. 10, 2006.
140. Supreme Court Decision 97Da13702 Decided Aug. 21, 1998.
141. Supreme Court Decision 96Da25500 Decided Apr. 28, 1998.
142. Supreme Court Decision 97Da16572 Decided Oct. 10, 1997.
143. Supreme Court Decision 2004Da63019 Decided Oct. 26, 2006.

grasps the relevance of business performance for the protection of victims who suffer harm caused by the employee. Therefore, according to this appearance theory, the relevance of business performance is determined in consideration of the degree of relationship between the employee's intended job and tortious acts and the employers' responsibility for risk creation and lack of preventive measures. Even in South Korean precedents, when an employee intentionally commits harm, such as sexually harassing or committing adultery with another employee.[144] Even when a taxi company's driver rapes a passenger, the relevance of business performance is widely recognized.[145] Therefore, the employer bears the responsibility for compensation to the victim. However, in case of transaction-related torts, if the victim knew that the employee's actions did not fall under the business performance or did not know through gross negligence, the relevance of the business performance is denied. Therefore, in this case, the employer is not liable to a third party for damage caused by the employee.[146]

106. According to the proviso to Article 756(1) of the Korean Civil Code, an employer may be exempted from liability for compensation to a third party if the employer has exercised due care in appointing the employee and supervising the performance of the specific affair. The burden of proving the duty of care in appointment and supervision is borne by the employer. South Korean Courts have not permitted employers to prove their immunity, so the employer's liability has been operated close to no-fault liability.

107. If the employer's liability for compensation is recognized pursuant to Article 756(1) of the Korean Civil Code, the employee shall bear the tort liability directly against the victim on the ground of his or her tortious act. The obligations of both parties are regarded as separate debts and are in a relationship of imperfect joint and several obligations.[147] However, the person who supervises the work of the employee on behalf of the employer is also responsible for the employer (Article 756(2) of the Korean Civil Code). This means, objectively, a person in a position to supervise a specific affair of business on behalf of an employer. For example, they are plant managers, field supervisors, etc. Even though the substitute supervisor bears the liability for compensation, the employer cannot escape the liability. Otherwise, if the employer is liable for compensation only when there is negligence in

144. Supreme Court Decision 2008Da89712 Decided Feb. 26, 2009. However, there is a case which denies the employer's liability (Supreme Court Decision 95Da39533 Decided Feb. 10, 1998).
145. Supreme Court Decision 90Da8954 Decided Jan. 11, 1991.
146. Supreme Court Decision 2003Da36133 Decided Feb. 25, 2005.
147. There is no explicit provision in the Korean Civil Code regarding the relationship of imperfect joint and several obligation. However, it is a relationship that is treated in accordance with the joint and several obligation by the Korean Civil Code. This is mainly recognized when several persons have tort liability to compensate the victim in separate tortious acts. According to the relationship of imperfect joint and several obligation, it is the same as in the case of joint and several obligation in which a large number of debtors have joint debt. Externally, the debtor bears the debt to perform the debt jointly to the creditors. However, this is different from the case of joint and several obligation. Between one creditor and one debtor, any cause other than payment, performance of goods, and deposit (e.g., a release of an obligation) does not affect the other debtor.

the appointment and supervision of the substitute supervisor, it will not protect the victim enough. It will also cause the result of giving an unfair advantage by shifting the risk of liability to the employer.[148]

If the employer compensates the victim for damage, he or she can claim reimbursement from the employee who is in a relationship of imperfect joint and several obligations. However, the employer's exercise of the right to indemnify the employee may be restricted. The South Korean Supreme Court held as follows. "These factors are taken into account: the nature and scale of the business, the current status of facilities, the contents of work and working conditions and working attitudes of employees, the cause and nature of the tortious act, duty of care of the employer regarding the prevention of the tortious act or distribution of losses, and other circumstances. Therefore, from the standpoint of equitable sharing of damages, the right to indemnity can be exercised against the employee only within a reasonable limit under the principle of good faith."[149]

§2. Independent Contractors

108. Article 757 of the Korean Civil Code stipulates that "The person who placed an order for a work to be done shall not be bound to make compensation for any damages caused to a third person by the contractor with respect to such work." Since the contractor bears the duty to complete the work in a position independent of the contractor, the person who placed an order for a work is not responsible for compensating for the harm caused by the contractor. However, in relation to the application of Article 757 or the relationship with Article 756 of the Korean Civil Code, the South Korean Supreme Court held as follows. "If the person who placed an order for a work has the right to command and supervise the work of the contractor, the relationship between the person who placed an order for a work and the contractor is practically no different from the relationship between the employer and the employee. Therefore, the person who placed an order for the work is liable for the employer's liability under article 756 of the Korean Civil Code."[150]

109. However, the person who placed an order for a work is liable for compensation if he or she was guilty of gross negligence in placing the order or in providing instructions therefor (Proviso of Article 757 of the Korean Civil Code). There are several explanations as to the purpose of this regulation. However, like the general tort liability requirements of Article 750 of the Korean Civil Code, it is considered that the person who placed an order for a work is responsible for his or her own negligence.[151]

148. *See* Kwak, Yoon-jik, *The Law of Obligations Law Special Part*, 421, 1995.
149. Supreme Court Decision 2009Da59350 Decided Nov. 26, 2009.
150. Supreme Court Decision 90Da18432 Decided Mar. 8, 1991.
151. For this reason, it has been pointed out that it is not appropriate for the proviso to Art. 757 of the Korean Civil Code to limit the liability of the person who placed an order for a work to "gross negligence."

§3. Liability of Legal Entities for Acts of Their Organs

110. Article 35(1) of the Korean Civil Code provides that a juristic person shall be liable for any damages done to other persons by its directors or other representatives in the performance of their duties. This stipulates the liability of the juristic person for the harm caused by the representative body. Responsibilities of a juristic person are stipulated by: (1) the actions of the representative body, (2) the performance relevance of the offending act, and (3) the general tortious acts of the representative body. In addition to directors, representative organizations that juristic persons should be responsible for in accordance with the above regulations include acting agents, special representatives, and liquidators. For the actions of non-representative organizations, juristic persons shall bear the employer's responsibilities under Article 756 of the Korean Civil Code.

111. In order to recognize the responsibility of a juristic person, the representative body's actions must have the performance relevance of business. It is sufficient if it can be viewed objectively as the performance of the representative agency in terms of whether it is related to the performance or not. Acts intended to promote the individual representative's personal interests may also be recognized as related performance. In addition, even when the representative agency violates laws and regulations related to the exercise of the right of representation and the act is invalidated, the tort liability of a juristic person may be recognized in relation to the other party.[152] For example, when a director of a school (juristic person) borrows money from a third party in the name of the school (juristic person) without obtaining permission from the supervisory authority for personal use, the South Korean Supreme Court held that such actions are invalid because they do not have permission from the supervisory authority. The Supreme Court explained that as a result, the third party suffered financial loss and such borrowing is related to the director's duties. Therefore, the school (juristic person) is liable for damages to a third party.[153] However, if the victim knows that the representative's actions do not correspond to the actions related to his/her duties, or if he/she does not know due to gross negligence, the corporation cannot be held liable for damages.

In order for corporate responsibility to be recognized, the representative body's actions must have job-related relevance. It is sufficient if it can be objectively regarded as the job act of the representative agency in terms of whether it is related to the job or not, and the act to promote the personal interest of the representative can also be recognized as job related. In addition, even if the representative agency violates laws and regulations related to the exercise of the right of representation and the act is invalidated, the liability of a corporation may be recognized in relation to the other party. For example, if a director of a school juristic person intends to use it for personal use and borrows money from a third party in the name of the school juristic person without permission from the supervisory authority, according to the Korean Supreme Court, such an act cannot be done without permission from the supervisory authority. It is invalid because of the relationship, and therefore, the

152. Supreme Court Decision 68Da2320 Decided Aug. 26, 1969.
153. Supreme Court Decision 86Da2534 Decided Apr. 28, 1987.

third party suffered financial damage. However, if the victim knows that the representative's actions do not correspond to the actions related to his or her duties, or if the victim does not know due to the victim's gross negligence, the juristic person is not liable for damages.[154]

112. A juristic person's tort liability can be recognized only when the representative agency's actions satisfy the tort liability requirements. Therefore, if the liability of a juristic person is recognized, the liability of the representative agency as an individual is also recognized. The two are in a relationship of imperfect joint and several obligations. However, if the act of a representative agency is beyond the scope of the purpose of the juristic person and cannot be recognized as an act of a juristic person (Article 34 of the Korean Civil Code), a juristic person is not liable for damage caused by the representative body. However, if any damage has been caused to other persons as a result of an ultra-vires act of a juristic person, those members, directors, and other representatives who have supported a resolution for such ultra-vires act or have carried it out are joint and severally liable for the damages caused thereby (Article 35(2) of the Korean Civil Code).

113. Article 755 of the Korean Civil Code provides that if a person who has caused any damage to another is exempt from liabilities under Article 753(Minor's Competency) or 754(Competency of Person of Mental Unsoundness), the person who is under a legal duty to supervise such person shall be liable to make compensation for the damage. This regulation establishes responsibility for those who have the duty to supervise the incompetent person for neglecting their supervisory duty. However, unlike general tort liability, the supervisor is not responsible for the damage caused by the person in charge of supervision but is responsible for the consequences of the damage by the incompetent person. In addition, the negligence of the person responsible for supervision is not the negligence of the person incapable of taking responsibility. Rather, it is the liability for the neglect of general supervision of the actions of incompetent persons.[155] In addition, according to the proviso to Article 755(1) of the Korean Civil Code, the burden of proof of negligence is shifted, and the responsibility for compensation cannot be avoided unless the supervisor proves that the supervisor was not negligent in supervision.

According to Article 755 of the Korean Civil Code, a person who bears the liability for compensation due to negligence of supervision is a person who bears the legal obligation to supervise a minor or a person who is a person of mental unsoundness. The person responsible for legal supervision of minors is the person with parental authority (Article 913 of the Korean Civil Code), the agent of parental authority (Articles 910 and 948 of the Korean Civil Code), and the guardian (Article 945 of the Korean Civil Code). In the case of a person of mental unsoundness, a guardian or a person responsible for supporting them becomes the person responsible for legal supervision (Article 39 of the Mental Health and Welfare Act). Substitute supervisors who will supervise the incompetent person on behalf of the

154. Supreme Court Decision 2005Da34711 Decided Jan. 18, 2008.
155. Seung-pyo, *The Commentary of Korean Civil Code—Law of Obligations (8)*, 81.

person responsible for legal supervision are the nanny of a daycare center and a kindergarten, the principal or teacher of an elementary school, and the director or doctor of a psychiatric hospital.

114. Supervisor's liability for compensation under Article 755 of the Korean Civil Code is based on the unlawfully tortious act of an incompetent person and negligence of supervisory duty. First, the supervisor's responsibility under Article 755 of the Korean Civil Code is that the incompetent person must have caused damage to others by objectively unlawfully tortious acts. Therefore, if the person's actions are not illegal due to reasons other than incapacity of responsibility, for example, grounds for exclusion of illegality such as self-defense, the supervisor's responsibility under Article 755 of the Korean Civil Code does not matter.[156] In addition, Article 755 of the Korean Civil Code applies only to cases where liability for compensation is not recognized due to incapacity in light of the contents of the law (supplemental nature). Accordingly, if a minor is liable for compensation himself, the supervisors' responsibility under Article 755 of the Korean Civil Code does not apply.[157]

Second, with respect to the negligence of the supervisory duty, the responsibility of the supervisory person is the responsibility of the parental authority for the minor. According to Article 913 of the Korean Civil Code, the person with parental authority has the duty to protect and educate children. Accordingly, they are also obligated to supervise minors so that they do not inflict damage on third parties. The content of the parental authority's duty to supervise minors must be specifically determined in each individual case. In this case, the age, maturity and development level of the minor, character and conduct, the predictability and risk of infringing behavior, and the possibility of avoiding damage by the person with parental authority are taken into consideration.[158] However, the duty of supervision of a person responsible for legal supervision does not matter whether he or she neglects to supervise the incompetent person in relation to the offense. Rather, the question is whether general supervision has been neglected throughout the life of the incompetent person. Also, since the burden of proof is shifted to the supervisor, it is extremely difficult to be exempted. The duty of supervision of the legal supervisor covers all aspects of the life relationship of minors and persons of mental unsoundness. However, the duties of a supervisor who supervises on behalf of the supervisor are limited in time and place. In addition, the content and scope of substitute supervisors are limited and specific compared to the supervisory duty of the legal supervisor.

Principals and teachers of schools or kindergartens are often treated as substitute supervisors. The South Korean Supreme Court has consistently held that: "The school principal or teacher's duty to protect and supervise students does not affect the student's entire life relationship within the school. It is limited to educational activities at school and life relationships that are closely inseparable from it. Even

156. Supreme Court Decision 77Da604 Decided Aug. 23, 1977.
157. South Korean courts and theories of scholars understand that general tort liability under Art. 750 of the Korean Civil Code can be applied to the above cases.
158. Seung-pyo, *The Commentary of Korean Civil Code—Law of Obligations (8)*, 433.

if it is a life relationship within the scope of the obligation, it is limited to cases where it is predicted that an accident can normally occur in school life or there is predictability (specific risk of occurrence of an accident). The principal or teacher shall be held responsible for the violation of the duty of protective supervision. Such predictability needs to be determined in consideration of the time and place of educational activities, the tortfeasor's ability to discern, the tortfeasor's acts, the relationship between the tortfeasor and the victim, and many other circumstances."[159] Even though the liability for compensation of the substitute supervisor is recognized, the person responsible for legal supervision cannot be exempted from liability for compensation to the victim simply because there is a substitute supervisor.[160]

115. Article 755 of the Korean Civil Code stipulates that the supervisor's liability for compensation can be established when the tortfeasor's liability for compensation is not recognized due to his or her incapacity. Therefore, conversely, if the minor has the capacity to take the tort responsibility, it can be considered that the supervisor's responsibility for compensation is not recognized. However, it was pointed out that this interpretation was unreasonable for the protection of victims. Korean precedents did not find a clear solution until the 1990s. Yet the South Korean Supreme Court held, "According to article 755 (1) of the Korean Civil Code, which is a special provision for article 750 of the Korean Civil Code, a person who has a statutory duty to supervise a minor who is unable to take responsibility is responsible for compensating for damages on the premise that the minor is not responsible. In this case, the responsibility cannot be avoided unless the person responsible for supervision proves that he has not neglected his or her supervisory duty. However, even though the minor has the capacity to take responsibility for the tort, if the damage has an adequate causation with the violation of the duty of supervisor, the person responsible for supervision is liable for damages as a general tortious offender."[161]

According to this Supreme Court Decision, the liability of the person responsible for supervision of the tortious acts of a responsible minor is different from that of Article 755 of the Korean Civil Code. Therefore, in accordance with the general principle of the Korean Civil Code, the victim bears the burden of proof for the violation of the supervisor's duty of care and the resulting damage. However, the supervisory duty of the legal supervisor for a responsible minor is also understood as a neglect of the general and daily supervisory duty, not a specific judgment on the offense. Therefore, it is structured as in the case of incompetent persons. When the minor's own liability for compensation is recognized, the supervisor and the minor, who are responsible in accordance with Article 750 of the Korean Civil Code, are jointly and severally liable for the damages.

---

159. Supreme Court Decision 92Da13646 Decided Feb. 12, 1993.
160. Supreme Court Decision 68Da1804 Decided Jan. 28, 1969; Supreme Court Decision 2005Da24318 Decided Apr. 26, 2007.
161. Supreme Court Decision 93Da13605 Decided Feb. 8, 1994.

116. Article 758(1) of the Korean Civil Code provides, "If any damages has been caused to another person by reason of any defect in the construction or maintenance of a structure, the person in possession of the structure shall be liable for such damages. Provided, That if the person in possession has exercised due care in order to prevent the occurrence of such damages, compensation for the damage shall be made by the owner." South Korea's liability of possessor, owner of structure is extended and applied to general corporate equipment that may cause damage. Therefore, it is different from what some countries recognize only in the case of fixtures on land, such as buildings. No-fault liability is recognized by the owner of the structure.

117. Liability for compensation under Article 758(1) of the Korean Civil Code is stipulated as the following conditions: (1) damage must have occurred from the structure; (2) defects in installation or preservation; (3) causation between the defect of the structure and the occurrence of damage; and (4) there is no reason for immunity.

First, a structure is an object manufactured by artificial work, such as fixtures on land, buildings, advertising towers, roads, bridges, etc. In addition, it includes physical equipment of the company, such as elevators, tools and machinery in buildings. The South Korean Supreme Court held that dynamic equipment such as a bullet truck is also included, and automobiles are also included in the structure.[162] Second, from the time the structure was installed or during the management process thereafter, the structure itself should not have had the safety that it should normally have according to its use. Whether or not a structure is defective is objectively determined on the basis of whether or not the duty to prevent risks to a degree generally required by social norms has been fulfilled in proportion to the risk of the structure. Compliance with laws and regulations should be considered in determining whether there is a defect or not. Therefore, if it does not meet the standards stipulated by laws and regulations, a defect in the structure may be recognized unless there are special circumstances. However, compliance with laws and regulations is not an absolute criterion.[163] Defects in a structure mean a condition in which the structure does not have the safety normally required according to its use. Therefore, it does not mean that it is always necessary to maintain the perfect condition in the installation and preservation of the structure. If an accident is caused as a result of an unusual action that is not in accordance with normal usage, the defect of the structure is not recognized.[164] It does not require the intention or negligence of the occupant or owner for defects. However, the victim bears the burden of proving the existence of a defect. However, the South Korean Supreme Court held that, for example, the roof of the building in question was blown down by the wind even

162. However, the Guarantee Of Automobile Accident Compensation Act is applied to damage caused by the operation of a motor vehicle.
163. Supreme Court Decision 97Da10444 Decided Jun. 24, 1997.
164. Supreme Court Decision 91Da37652 Decided Apr. 24, 1992.

though there was nothing wrong with other buildings nearby. Therefore, it is determined that the accident can be presumed to be due to a defect in the structure.[165] Therefore, the burden of proof on the victim is eased.

The third requirement for structure liability is that there must be a causation between the defect and damage to the structure. Therefore, if the damage is caused by force majeure regardless of the defect of the structure, immunity from the structure's responsibility can be recognized. However, if it is recognized that there is a defect, damage caused by the defect is presumed. Therefore, even if the damage occurred due to force majeure of a natural disaster and there was no defect, the person liable for compensation bears the burden of proof for unavoidable circumstances. The South Korean Supreme Court held that concentrated torrential rain was an unusual natural phenomenon that could not normally be predicted in the accident area. However, it cannot be concluded that there was force majeure just by the fact that there was heavy rain, unless it is recognized that the collapse of the cutoff site could not have been prevented even if the necessary facilities were equipped for road safety.[166] Fourth, the reason for immunity should not be recognized. The occupant of the structure may be relieved of liability by proving that he or she has not neglected the care necessary to prevent damage. For example, the previous lessee carried out the interior work on the ceiling of the leased building, so it was impossible to know whether the ceiling was abnormal from the outside. In that case, it was acknowledged that the lessee who leased the building could not foresee and prevent any hidden defects in the ceiling. In this case, immunity of the occupant of the structure was granted.[167] In case the occupant of the structure is granted immunity, the owner of the structure is not exempted from liability for damages as long as the defect in the structure and damage resulting therefrom are recognized.

118. Liability for damages due to defects in the structure is primarily borne primarily by the possessor of the structure. If the possessor proves that he or she has taken the necessary precautions to prevent damage, the possessor is liable for the damages secondarily. While acknowledging the primary responsibility of the possessor who actually uses and manages the structure, the content of the owner's responsibility is strictly aggravated. However, if there is a defect in planting or preservation of trees, and damage is caused by the defect, the possessor or owner of a tree has the same responsibilities as the possessor or owner of the structure.

119. Article 759(1) of the Korean Civil Code provides, "Every possessor of an animal is liable for any loss inflicted on a third person by the animal: Provided, That this shall not apply where the possessor has not been negligent in giving due care in taking custody of the animal according to the species and nature of the animal." This regulation also shifts the burden of proof for the duty of care, similar to the responsibility of the supervisor and the employer, so that the owner of the animal can prove the reason for immunity. In some countries, liability for compensation differs depending on whether it is a livestock. However, in South Korea, there are

165. Supreme Court Decision 74Da246 Decided Nov. 26, 1974.
166. Supreme Court Decision 83DaKa348 Decided Aug. 24, 1982.
167. Supreme Court Decision 83DaKa2266 Decided Mar. 13, 1984.

no different regulations according to the type of livestock. Due care in the storage of animals borne by the owners of animals should be determined concretely according to the type, nature, and surrounding circumstances of the animal in a specific case. For example, the owner of a big Tosa dog with a high risk of harming people has a duty of care. Thus, he or she must check whether there is a safe facility to manage and store the Tosa dog and when he or she lends the potentially dangerous dog to someone. If the owner neglects this duty of care and lends it to someone who does not have a separate kennel and ties the dog with an old leash and causes an accident, the owner cannot avoid liability for compensation for violating the duty of care to prevent accidents.[168]

168. Supreme Court Decision 80DaKa2966 Decided Feb. 10, 1981.

Part III. Forms of Strict Liability

Chapter 1. Road and Traffic Accidents

120. In relation to damage accidents caused by high-speed transportation, in South Korea, the liability of the holder is stipulated in the relevant laws depending on the transportation organization that caused the accident. The Guarantee Of Automobile Accident Compensation Act stipulates the no-negligence liability of car owners for accidents resulting from the operation of automobiles. In the case of damage to goods or passengers in the course of land transportation by rail, Articles 135 and 148 of the Korean Commercial Code[169] stipulate the carrier's liability for damages. In addition, Articles 796, 798 and 826 of the Korean Commercial Code stipulate for personal and material damage related to the ship or its operation. Article 899 of the Korean Commercial Code also stipulates strict liability for carriers with respect to the liability of air carriers for air transport.

121. Civil liability for automobile accidents is divided into driver liability under the Korean Civil Code and motor vehicle owner liability under the Guarantee Of Automobile Accident Compensation Act. The driver's liability is the responsibility to compensate for damage caused to others by the failure of the driver of the vehicle to fulfill his or her duty of care. Depending on whether the driver has a contractual relationship with the victim, the driver's liability for breach of contract and tort liability arises.[170] However, the motor vehicle owner is to bear no-fault liability under the Guarantee Of Automobile Accident Compensation Act in the case of inflicting death or personal damage on another person due to the operation of the vehicle.

122. No matter how careful the driver is when driving a car, accidents cannot be avoided. Even in such cases, victims of accidents must be promptly and sufficiently remedied. In order to achieve this purpose, the Guarantee Of Automobile Accident Compensation Act imposes no-fault liability on the motor vehicle owner who manages and controls the operation of the automobile because he or she enjoys the benefits of operating the automobile.

---

169. Korea Legislation Research Institute translates its title as "Commercial Act." However, these authors understand "Commercial Code" would be proper in comparative law perspective.

170. The carrier's liability for damages under Arts. 135 and 148 of the Korean Commercial Code applies to carriers whose business is transportation using automobiles. And to that extent, the provisions of the Korean Commercial Code take precedence over the liability provisions of the Korean Civil Code.

As introduced below, the liability of a motor vehicle owner under the Guarantee Of Automobile Accident Compensation Act applies to "personal harm," which is the death or injury of any person (Article 3 of the Guarantee Of Automobile Accident Compensation Act). The Guarantee Of Automobile Accident Compensation Act takes precedence over the Korean Civil Code as a special law. Therefore, if the victim asks the motor vehicle owner for compensation under the Guarantee Of Automobile Accident Compensation Act, the liability for compensation under the Korean Civil Code doesn't matter. Meanwhile, the Guarantee Of Automobile Accident Compensation Act compels motor vehicle owners to purchase liability insurance to pay compensation to victims of personal and material damage (Article 5 of the Guarantee Of Automobile Accident Compensation Act). With regard to personal and material damage exceeding the limit of liability insurance, breach of contract or tort liability under the Korean Civil Code is an issue (Article 4 of the Guarantee Of Automobile Accident Compensation Act, Articles 390, 750, and 756 of the Korean Civil Code).

123. The liability of a motor vehicle owner under Article 3 of the Guarantee Of Automobile Accident Compensation Act shall be: (1) to operate a motor vehicle for personal use, (2) to cause an accident due to the operation of the car, (3) to kill or injure person, and (4) there is no reason for immunity. The first requirement for liability is to operate a motor vehicle. The term "operation" means using or managing motor vehicles according to their usage, regardless of whether they transport persons or carry items. The person who enjoys the profits while controlling and managing the operation of such a motor vehicle is the motor vehicle operator. A motor vehicle operator does not mean a driver who actually drives or assists in driving a vehicle. Also, a motor vehicle operator is largely the same as the vehicle owner, i.e., the owner of the vehicle or the person who has the right to use the vehicle. However, such as a person driving a stolen vehicle may have the status of a driver, although he or she is not a vehicle owner. Those who rent cars for a fee, such as car rental companies, automobile driving schools, automobile maintenance mechanics, and those who steal automobiles without asking whether the driver's rights are legal or not. They are motor vehicle operators who enjoy control over the operation of a vehicle and enjoy operating profits. The South Korean Supreme Court has recognized the motor vehicle operators as follows: a person who has delivered the vehicle while receiving the full payment and issuing all necessary documents for the transfer of the registered name but has not yet completed the transfer registration;[171] a person who rents a car free of charge to a family member or friend;[172] the owner of the pub, which is in charge of car and car keys from customers.[173] However, a passenger who rides for free in a car driven by another person, a substitute driver who receives payment from the owner of the vehicle and temporarily takes the place of driving, does not have the status of a car operator.

171. Supreme Court Decision 91Da28177 Decided Jun. 23, 1992.
172. Supreme Court Decision 87DaKa376 Decided Jan. 10, 1987.
173. Supreme Court Decision 97DaKa35115 Decided Dec. 26, 1997.

124. The second requirement for liability of the motor vehicle operator is that the accident must have occurred due to the operation of the vehicle. The term "operation" means using or managing motor vehicles according to their usage, regardless of whether they transport persons or carry items. The use according to the usage of the vehicle is not limited to the case of operating the motor and driving device. Therefore, it is understood as the use of all devices installed in automobiles, such as car doors, cranes, and dumps. Thus, for example, after transporting a patient to a hospital by an ambulance and disembarking the patient with an extra bed provided in the ambulance, it is considered an accident while driving, even if the patient is accidentally dropped and injured by dropping the patient on the ground.[174] However, while sleeping with the ignition and heater turned on in a motor vehicle for the purpose of cold protection while using it as a sleeping space, a person dies due to suffocation. In this case, the South Korean Supreme Court held that the damage caused by suffocation was an accident that occurred regardless of the nature or danger of a vehicle as a means of transportation and did not constitute an accident of operating a motor vehicle.[175] In addition, the occurrence of damage to the human body of another person is a condition for establishing liability. "Other person" means any person other than the driver of the vehicle that caused the accident and the driver at fault (including the driver's assistant). A passenger who rides for free in a car driven by another person is "another person."

125. With regard to the reason for exemption, the Guarantee Of Automobile Accident Compensation Act distinguishes between the case of the death or injury of any person other than a passenger and the case of death or injury of a passenger. In cases of the death or injury of any person other than a passenger, the motor vehicle operator is not liable for the damage when it has been proven that: (1) the person who has operated the motor vehicle and the driver thereof were not negligent in its operation, (2) that a victim or a third party, other than the person who has operated the motor vehicle and the driver thereof, commits an intentional or negligent act, and (3) that there were no structural defects or functional disorders in the motor vehicle.

In cases of the death or injury of a passenger, the motor vehicle operator can only be exempted from liability if he or she proves that the passenger has died or been injured due to the passenger's intentional act or suicidal act. Thus, the motor vehicle operator cannot avoid liability for compensation on the ground that he or she is not at fault. The intentional or suicidal act of the passenger is limited to the act made consciously based on the free decision-making of the passenger.[176] It is understood that such a regulatory attitude introduces the legal principle of strict liability, unlike general tort liability for automobile accidents.

126. The liability of the motor vehicle operator is recognized for personal damage caused by a motor vehicle accident. If the liability for compensation is recognized, the victim can claim the damage, which is in adequate causation to the

174. Supreme Court Decision 2004DaKa20340, 20357 Decided Jul. 9, 2004.
175. Supreme Court Decision 99Da41824 Decided Jan. 21, 2000.
176. Supreme Court Decision 95Da22115 Decided Nov. 11, 1997.

accident. Therefore, the damages that the victim can claim include positive damages, such as medical expenses, and adverse damages, such as lost income. Also, pain and suffering damages are included.

In any of the following cases, the Government shall, in response to a claim filed by a victim, compensate for damage sustained by the victim to the extent and amount covered by liability insurance: (1) where a victim has died or been injured due to an accident that occurred during the operation of a motor vehicle, the owner of which is unidentified. (2) where a person other than a policyholder is liable to compensate for damage (Article 30 of the Guarantee Of Automobile Accident Compensation Act).

The amount of liability insurance that a motor vehicle owner must purchase is KRW 150 million in the case of death on a per-victim basis, and in case of injury, up to KRW 30 million depending on the severity of the injury. And for the sequelae that remain after the treatment of the injury, it is recognized within the range of up to KRW 150 million depending on the contents of the disability.

127. The Korean Commercial Code stipulates liability for material and personal damage to a person whose business is transportation. A carrier is liable for damage resulting from the loss of, damage to or delay in the delivery of goods unless he or she proves that the carrier, forwarding agents, his or her employees, or other persons employed in respect of the carriage did not fail to exercise due care in connection with the receipt, delivery, custody, and carriage of the goods (Article 135 of the Korean Commercial Code). A carrier cannot be exonerated from liability for damage received in the carriage of passengers unless he or she proves that he/she or his/her employees have not neglected to exercise due care in connection with the carriage (Article 148 of the Korean Commercial Code). The land carrier's liability for compensation is understood to be based on the contract of carriage, and the carrier's negligence is presumed. Therefore, the carrier can prove that he or she has not neglected his duty of care and can be exempted.

In practice, however, the carrier's immunity has rarely been granted. For example, the South Korean Supreme Court held in the case of loss of shipment due to robbery, "It cannot be said that it is itself a reason for immunity due to force majeure. Therefore, it is necessary to determine again whether there was no cause attributable to the carrier or its employees. In that case, it was judged that the no fault of the carrier or the employee could not be inferred based on the rule of thumb."[177] In the case of shipping by sea, if a carrier does not prove that he/she, the crew or other employees of a ship have exercised due care concerning the receipt, loading, stowage, transportation, storage, unloading and delivery of cargo, he or she shall be liable to compensate for the damage incurred due to loss of, damage to or late arrival of the cargo (Article 795 of the Korean Commercial Code). Exemption may be granted if it is proved that the damage to the transport was caused by force majeure, piracy, or hidden defects in the transport (Article 796 of the Korean Commercial Code). The strict liability of such maritime carriers is fixed and limited to a certain amount of compensation. The contents of liability identified as contractual liability also apply to liability for compensation due to the tort of the carrier due to

177. Supreme Court Decision 98Da9038 Decided Dec. 10, 1999.

loss of goods (Article 798 of the Korean Commercial Code). The provisions on the liability of the maritime carrier for the loss of goods are applied mutatis mutandis to cases where damage is inflicted to the passenger in the course of the transportation of the sea passenger (Article 826 of the Korean Commercial Code). Also, in the case of air transport, the Korean Commercial Code requires the carrier to be liable for compensation for personal damage to passengers, regardless of negligence, if it occurs on the aircraft or during the work for the lift (Article 904 of the Korean Commercial Code). Even in the case of damage caused by loss or damage to the transported goods during transport, compensation shall be made unless it is proved that the transport was caused by defects or force majeure (Article 913 of the Korean Commercial Code). The liability of air carriers, which is a no-fault liability, is recognized as limited to a certain amount (Articles 905 and 915 of the Korean Commercial Code). This contractual liability applies to the liability for damages caused by the tort of the air carrier, as in the case of sea transportation (Article 899 of the Korean Commercial Code).

Chapter 2. Product Liability

128. In South Korea, as industrialization began in earnest in the 1970s, accidents caused by defects in manufacturing became a frequent problem. In the process, academic studies and case law on civil liability for defects in products have also been steadily accumulating.

At the same time, in response to the global trend for unification of product liability in the 1990s and the steady request of domestic academics, the Product Liability Act was enacted in South Korea in 2001. At the time of legislation, (1) title of legislation (manufacturer responsibility, producer responsibility, manufactured liability, product liability); (2) method of regulation of product liability (negligence liability, strict liability); (3) scope of product (whether including real estate, agricultural products, electricity/gas, software); (4) regulation method (classification of types) regarding product defects were mainly discussed. Consequently, it has been enacted as described below. The main characteristics of product liability under the South Korean Product Liability Act are: (a) that it is a non-contractual liability that does not ask whether there is a contractual relationship between the victim and the manufacturer; (b) that it is the responsibility of compensating for damage to life, body or property due to a defect in the product; (c) that it is the strict liability. Thus, it is irrelevant, whether the manufacturer is at fault. The Product Liability Act has the character of a special law that corrects the tort liability of the Korean Civil Code, which has the principle of negligence. Unless otherwise specified in the Product Liability Act, the provisions of the Korean Civil Code are applied (Article 8 of the Product Liability Act). One of the provisions of the Korean Civil Code applied to the Product Liability Act is the provision of the scope of damages (Article 393 of the Korean Civil Code). According to Article 393 of the Korean Civil Code, the victim's damage is stipulated to compensate for ordinary damage and for damage caused by special circumstances that the tortfeasor can individually foresee. In other words, the South Korean Product Liability Act, unlike some countries, does not follow the position which sets an upper limit on the amount of damages.

129. Before the Product Liability Act was enacted in South Korea, damage to a victim due to a defect in a product was regulated as liability for breach of contract (Article 390 of the Korean Civil Code) when there was a contractual relationship between the victim and the tortfeasor. And if there was no contractual relationship, it was regulated as liability for damages under general tort liability (Article 750 of the Korean Civil Code). In determining whether tort liability was established, the manufacturer's negligence for defects in the product was important. In addition, the causation between the defect in the product and the damage to the victim became the key issue for remedies for the victim. In this regard, the South Korean Supreme Court ruled as follows in the so-called Chicken Feed Case, in which feed contained impurities, which significantly lowered the egg-laying rate of chickens and caused property damage to poultry farmers. "Some impurities were contained in the compound feed and the basic feed, and as a result of the feeding test with the above feed, the same test results were shown. There was no problem with the feeding method, house management, or feed storage. Also, the feed provided for the breeding test was not decomposed or spoiled. And there was nothing wrong with the method or drug of the Newcastle vaccination that was given to the chickens when they were feeding the feed. Therefore, at least the feed must have contained some impurities, and there was a negligence in the manufacturing process. If the chickens raised by the plaintiff cause the above phenomenon, the seller of the feed manufacturing and selling is liable for the tortious act."[178] It assumes the manufacturer's negligence for a defect in the product. In addition, the burden of proving the causation between the defect and the occurrence of damage was alleviated if there were no other errors in feed management and usage methods.

This attitude continued in subsequent cases, and even now, when the Product Liability Act based on no-fault liability is enacted, the court rule of alleviating the burden of proof on the victim in relation to causation has been maintained.

130. The Product Liability Act takes strict responsibility that does not require the manufacturer's negligence as a requirement, and the scope of application is "product." The term "product" means movables which are industrially manufactured or processed including movables incorporated into other movables or immovables (Article 2 No. 1 of the Product Liability Act). As long as it is movable, it does not have to be a finished product, and the Product Liability Act also applies to parts and raw materials. In addition, the Product Liability Act applies not only to new products but also to used and remanufactured products. As the Product Liability Act applies to "manufactured or processed personal property," it does not apply to intangible services, unprocessed agricultural products, or real estate. Whether information or software is a product has been controversial since the legislative session. Although there are opinions that affirm it, many views of South Korean scholars deny it because they are not natural forces that can be managed. When software is stored and distributed in a fixed storage medium such as a USB or semiconductor chip, there is no consensus on whether it is a product as a part of the storage medium.

The subject of liability under the Product Liability Act is the manufacturer. The manufacturer is a person who engages in the business of manufacturing or importing and processing of products. It also includes those who use their name, firm name, trademark or any other discernible sign on a product trade name, trademark or other identifiable symbol on their products to identify themselves as a manufacturer or to make such a mark that may lead to misunderstanding (label manufacturer) (Article 2, No. 3 of the Product Liability Act). A person who engages in the manufacturing and processing of products as a business means a person who repeats and continues such activities, which do not necessarily mean profit-making. Therefore, public institutions or nonprofit corporations that provide products free of charge can also be the subject of compensation for product liability. In addition, importers who bring products from abroad into Korea are recognized as the same subject of responsibility as manufacturers.

Label manufacturers using the Original Equipment Manufacturing (OEM) method or the PB (Private Brand) method are also designated as the subject of liability for the protection of victims. Furthermore, if the manufacturer of the product is unknown, the person who supplied the product for profit by selling or leasing

178. Supreme Court Decision 75Da2092 Decided Jan. 25, 1977.

it is liable for compensation. However, the supplier may be exempted from liability by informing the injured person of the manufacturer of the product or the supplier within a reasonable period upon request from the injured (Article 3(2) of the Product Liability Act).

131. The manufacturer's liability for damages under the Product Liability Act is subject to the following requirements: (1) defects in the product, (2) damages due to defects in the product, and (3) no exemption (Article 3 of the Product Liability Act).

First, a product defect means that the product lacks safety, which can ordinarily be expected of a product (Article 2, No. 2 of the Product Liability Act). The purpose of the Product Liability Act is to compensate for damage to the life, body, and property of the victim due to the product. Therefore, defects in the product are also identified as dangerous states that can cause damage to the life, body, or property of the user of the product.

This is distinct from product defects, such as product quality abnormalities. Defects in products are a key requirement of the Product Liability Act, which corresponds to the fault of the manufacturer in the negligence principle. It should be determined whether the product has the expected safety in light of the current technological level and economic feasibility in the structure, quality, and performance of the product.[179] Regarding product defects, the Product Liability Act categorizes defects into defects in manufacturing, defects in design, and defects in indication, according to the global trend.

132. Defect in anufacturing means that the product has become unsafe because it is manufactured or processed differently from the original design. It does not ask whether the manufacturer has fulfilled his or her duty of care in manufacturing and processing the product. These manufacturing defects are caused by the use of defective raw materials, the use of insufficient or inadequate manufacturing equipment, insufficient inspection or the adoption of inappropriate inspection methods. A defect in design is a case in which the product is defective because the alternative design was not adopted, even though the damage or risk could have been avoided or reduced if the manufacturer had adopted a reasonable alternative design. In the cases of sudden automobile acceleration[180] and tobacco lawsuits,[181] the Supreme Court of South Korea held concerning design flaws, "following factors should be determined in the light of social norms by comprehensively considering various circumstances: characteristics and uses of the product; content of users's expectations

179. Regarding this general content in South Korean literature, it is understood that it is necessary to determine whether a product is defective by comprehensively considering the various factors suggested in Art. 6 of the European Community's Directive on Product Liability of Jul. 25, 1985, Directive 85/374/EEC, O.J.EC 1985 L 210/29. These factors are: (1) the usefulness of the product compared to the frequency and magnitude of the risk; (2) the probability and severity of the damage; (3) the timing of the supply of the product by the manufacturer or supplier; (4) the use and form of use of the product, (5) the technical and economic feasibility of designing and labeling to prevent danger, etc.

180. Supreme Court Decision 2003Da16771 Decided Mar. 12, 2004.

181. Supreme Court Decision 2011Da22092 Decided Apr. 10, 2014.

for the product; content of anticipated risks; user perception of risks; possibility of avoiding risks by users; possibility of alternative designs and economic costs; the relative strengths and weaknesses of the adopted design and the alternative design." A defect in indication means a case where the damage or risk that may occur due to the product could be reduced or avoided, but this was not done if the manufacturer had provided a reasonable explanation, instruction, warning, or other indication. Violation of duty of explanation or duty of indication or warning is understood as a type of defect. Even if defects in manufacturing or design are not recognized, product liability for defects in indication may be recognized. In the tobacco litigation case, the South Korean Supreme Court ruled that "It should be determined whether there is a defect in the labeling in consideration of various factors: the characteristics of the product; the type of use normally used; the contents of users' expectations for the product; the contents of expected risks; the users' perception of risks and the possibility of avoiding by the users."[182]

133. The second requirement for liability under the Product Liability Act is that damage to life, body, or property would have occurred due to a defect in the product. Matters concerning any liability for damages caused by the defect of a product are governed by the Korean Civil Code except as otherwise provided for in the Product Liability Act (Article 8 of the Product Liability Act). Therefore, in South Korea, it is understood that non-economic damage caused by a defect in the product is also included in the scope of compensation. However, if the damage to the victim occurs only for the product, the Product Liability Act does not apply, as Article 3 of the Product Liability Act makes clear. Damage caused to the product itself due to the lack of product suitability is identified as an area to be regulated by contractual liability, such as liability for warranty against defect. This rule was recognized even before the introduction of the Product Liability Act.[183] What is controversial is whether or not product liability law protects against pure property damage, such as loss of business due to a defect in a product. According to the theory of Korean scholars, the product liability law in South Korea does not limit the damage to be compensated, so damage to pure property is also included. However, the Supreme Court of South Korea held "Property damage only to a product," to which the Product Liability Act does not apply, includes not only property damage to the product itself but also damage caused by business loss caused by defects in the product. "However, this is not subject to the product liability law."[184]

134. In order to admit product liability, the causation must be recognized between the defect in the product and the occurrence of damage. The Product Liability Act does not provide a separate provision for proof of causation. Consequently, in accordance with the general principles of the Korean Civil Code, the victim must assert and prove the causation. Regarding the proof of causation in product liability, even before the introduction of the Product Liability Act, it was already

182. Supreme Court Decision 2011Da22092 Decided Apr. 10, 2014.
183. Supreme Court Decision 97Da26593 Decided Feb. 5, 1999.
184. Supreme Court Decision 2003Da16771 Decided Mar. 12, 2004; Supreme Court Decision 2005Da31361 Decided Mar. 10, 2006.

intended to alleviate the difficulty of proving the victim in the application of tort liability under Article 750 of the Korean Civil Code. Even after the introduction of the Product Liability Act, the South Korean Supreme Court ruled as follows. "In the case of imposing liability for damages on the manufacturer due to a defect in a product that is mass-produced with high technology intensive, the production process of the product is known only to the manufacturer who is an expert, so that there is a peculiarity that the general public cannot reveal what kind of defect existed in the product and whether damage occurred due to the defect. Therefore, it is extremely difficult for the consumer to prove the causation scientifically and technically between the defect in the product and the occurrence of the damage. Thus, in the case of an accident under normal use of the product, ① if the consumer proves that the accident occurred in an area under the exclusive control of the manufacturer, and that the accident does not normally occur without the fault of a person, ② unless the manufacturer can prove that the accident occurred due to a cause other than the defect in the product, it can be presumed that the defect exists in the product and that the accident occurred due to the defect." In this way, the victim's burden of proof is alleviated.[185]

135. According to the Product Liability Act, even if damage occurred due to a defect in the product, the liability for compensation is exempted if a person who is liable for damages proves any of the following facts:

(1) That the manufacturer did not supply the product.
(2) That the existence of the defect could not be identified by the state of scientific or technical knowledge of the time when the manufacturer supplied the product (so-called development risk defense).
(3) That the defect is attributable to the manufacturer who complied with the standard prescribed by any Act or subordinate statute of the time when he or she supplied the product.
(4) In the case of raw materials or components, the defect is attributable to the design or the instruction on manufacturing by the manufacturer of the product made of the relevant raw materials or components.

However, regarding the above reasons for exemption, the manufacturer's claim for immunity is limited in certain cases. For example, in the case of development risk defense, the obligation of the manufacturer to monitor the product *ex post* is recognized in order to prevent damage due to defects in the product even after distribution of the product. Therefore, if the manufacturer does not properly fulfill the follow-up monitoring obligation, the product liability cannot be waived by using the reason for exemption. However, any special agreement that excludes or limits liability for damages under the Product Liability Act is invalid (Article 6 of the Product Liability Act).

185. Supreme Court Decision 2003Da16771 Decided Mar. 12, 2004; Supreme Court Decision 2005Da31361 Decided Mar. 10, 2006.

136. The right of claim for damages under the Product Liability Act is extinguished by the completion of prescription if the injured person or his/her legal representative does not exercise his/her rights within three years from the date on which the injured person or his/her legal representative becomes aware of both of the following facts: damage and the person liable for the damage (Article 7(1) of the Product Liability Act). The right of claim for damages under this Act shall be exercised within ten years from the date on which the manufacturer supplied the product which caused the relevant damages, provided that with respect to damages caused by any substances which are accumulated in the body and, in turn, hurt the relevant person's health, or any other damages the symptoms of which appear after a lapse of a certain latent period, the aforesaid period shall be reckoned from the date on which the damage occurs actually (Article 7(2) of the Product Liability Act).

137. Since the enactment of product liability, significant cases on whether to recognize product liability have been issued several times in South Korea. There are cases on whether defects in design and in indication of automobiles are issues in relation to automobile sudden acceleration accidents.[186] In a case where a person who took a cold medicine called "Contact 600" died of a hemorrhagic stroke, the judgment was made on whether the manufacturing of the drug using a synthetic chemical called phenylpropanolamine, which is known to cause it, was a defect in the product.[187] Also, in a case where a hemophilia patient became infected with HIV after receiving blood products, the South Supreme Court held the rule on the estimation of the causation between a defect in a drug and infection so that the victim can receive sufficient compensation for damages in relation to the application of the Product Liability Act in the pharmaceutical field.[188] In addition, in relation to the application of the Product Liability Act to the damage caused by defoliants of Vietnam War veterans, defects in products due to the inclusion of hazardous substances were recognized. However, the South Korean Supreme Court required the factors necessary to recognize the causation between the defect and nonspecific diseases such as diabetes to specify the epidemiological causation. However, the Supreme Court makes clear that a proportional causal relationship is unacceptable.[189] The rule on the recognition of product liability according to epidemiological causation was reexamined in the cases of Lung cancer caused by smoking[190] and of an automobile manufacturer on the grounds that asthma was onset or worsened due to automobile exhaust gas.[191]

---

186. Supreme Court Decision 2003Da16771 Decided Mar. 12, 2004; As cases before the enforcement of the Product Liability Act, Supreme Court Decision 2001Da44659 Decided Nov. 27, 2001.
187. Supreme Court Decision 2007Da52287 Decided Feb. 28, 2008 (The Supreme Court denies the application of Product Liability Act in this case.).
188. Supreme Court Decision 2008Da16776 Decided Sep. 29, 2011. Also, in the cases where calves died after using the vaccine, the Supreme Court negated the defect in the product. They are Supreme Court Decision 2011Da88870 Decided Sep. 26, 2013; Supreme Court Decision 2013Da26708, 26733, 26739 Decided Nov. 9, 2017.
189. Supreme Court Decision 2006Da17539 Decided Jul. 12, 2013; Supreme Court Decision 2006Da17553 Decided Jul. 12, 2013.
190. Supreme Court Decision 2011Da22092 Decided Apr. 10, 2014.
191. Supreme Court Decision 2011Da7437 Decided Sep. 4, 2014.

Chapter 3. Liability for Service

138. In South Korea, there is no strict liability for labor or services. The product liability Act does not apply to services. In addition, if damage is caused to a customer or a third party in the process of providing services such as installation of the product, breach of contract or tort liability can only be recognized on the ground of a labor provider's breach of due diligence.[192] However, if the provision of service is directly related to the product, for example, in the process of storing blood by refrigeration or chemical treatment or extracting and processing only some components of blood to make blood products, strict liability for compensation is recognized in accordance with the Product Liability Act for damage resulting from the defect.

192. In case of being responsible for the installation work of fixing the completed and delivered generator to the construction site, the South Korean Supreme Court held that since it does not fall under the manufacturer of the generator, so that it cannot be the subject of liability for damages under the Product Liability Act. Supreme Court Decision 2012Da4824 Decided Mar. 26, 2015.

Chapter 4. Environmental Liability

139. As the basis for liability for compensation for damage caused by environmental pollution, there is Article 750 of the Korean Civil Code stipulating tortious acts, Article 758 of the Korean Civil Code on liability for structures, and various environmental-related special laws. Also, there is "Act On Liability For Environmental Damage And Relief Thereof," which has been in effect since 2016 and stipulates no-fault liability. In addition to liability for damages, Articles 13 and 14 of "the Act On Liability For Environmental Damage And Relief Thereof" recognize the measures of restoration to the original state as an *ex post* remedy. An injunction for prohibition of environmental pollution can be filed in the form of a right to claim for removal and prevention of disturbance based on ownership (Article 214[193] of the Korean Civil Code) or a right to request a prohibition of disturbance against adjoining land by soot, etc. (Article 217[194] of the Korean Civil Code). Below, we will introduce South Korean environmental responsibility, focusing on tort liability under Article 750 of the Korean Civil Code and "the Act On Liability For Environmental Damage And Relief Thereof."

140. In South Korea, the discussion of civil liability for environmental pollution began in the 1970s, when industrialization and the accompanying pollution problem emerged. The starting point of the discussion was the content of judgment of illegality and negligence, which are the requirements for establishing general tort liability under Article 750 of the Korean Civil Code for harm caused by pollution. At that time, there was also an opinion that environmental pollution itself was illegal by stating environmental rights. However, in general, it was judged that environmental pollution itself cannot be said to be illegal, and whether or not it is illegal can be determined by comparing the nature and degree of the infringed profit and the mode of the infringement (so-called tolerance limit theory). This position also influenced Korean cases. Korean courts have determined its illegality after comprehensively considering all circumstances, such as the degree of damage, the nature of damage benefits and social evaluation, the use of the damaging building, locality, the precedence of land use, the possibility of preventing and avoiding damage.[195]

---

193. Article 214 (Claim for Removal and Prevention of Disturbance against Article Owned):

> An owner may demand the cessation of disturbance from a person who disturbs ownership, and may demand either prevention of the disturbance or security for damages from the person who might disturb ownership.

194. Article 217 (Prohibition of Disturbance against Adjoining Land by Soot, etc.):

> (1) The owner of land has a duty to take appropriate measures so that soot, heat gas, liquid, sound, vibration, and the like may not harm or disturb the neighbor's living or use of the adjoining land.
> (2) If the situation under the preceding paragraph is appropriate for the ordinary use of the adjoining land, the neighbor has the duty of enduring such a situation.

195. Supreme Court Decision 98Da56997 Decided May 16, 2000; Supreme Court Decision 2003Da64602 Decided Sep. 13, 2004.

At this time, compliance with public law regulations should also be considered in determining illegality, but even if it is suitable for administrative law regulations, it has been judged that if the degree of interference exceeds the level of tolerance in social life, it can be evaluated as an illegal act.[196] With regard to negligence, the South Korean Supreme Court held, "It cannot be said that there was no negligence on the ground that the defendant had modern science facilities to prevent damage in all possible ways at the time of establishment or operation of the factory."[197] Thus, the negligence was strictly determined. Recently, the South Korean Supreme Court held that if the degree of harm exceeds the normal tolerance limit and causes damage, the liability for damages cannot be avoided.[198] Therefore, it is judged by mixing illegality and negligence depending on whether the limit is exceeded.

141. Liability for tort due to environmental pollution is recognized only when there is a causation between environmental pollution and damage. The burden of proof is, in principle, borne by the victim. In this regard, early South Korean Court cases did not adopt the rule that the causation in a pollution case is prima facie presumed to be litigationally proven if there is a probability that the causation can be inferred, unlike general torts.[199] However, later, the South Korean Supreme Court held, "With respect to the causation in the tortious act caused by pollution, if there is a probability that the result would not have occurred without the tortious act, it would be sufficient. In other words, it would be enough to prove that there is a considerable possibility that the causation exists between the infringement and the damage."

"The tortfeasor can only deny the causation if he or she disproves it. While maintaining the conventional principle of burden of proof that the plaintiff claiming damages has the burden of proof, this alleviates or reduces the scope of the victim's proof. On the other hand, it is reasonable to accept the probability theory, which aims to expand the scope of the tortfeasor's disproving evidence." This eased the burden of proving the causation of the victim.[200] After that, this rule has developed into the name of the so-called new probability theory, which specifies the elements that each party must assert and prove.

"It is appropriate to the concept of social equity to say that if any harmful causative substances emitted by the tortfeasor reach the injured parties' goods and cause damage, tortfeasor cannot escape liability unless the tortfeasor proves that it is harmless."

In this case, which is a pollution lawsuit due to water pollution, the South Korean Supreme Court held, "① Wastewater that can adversely affect the growth of seaweed is discharged from the defendant factory; ② Some of the wastewater reached the seaweed farm in this case through oil; ③ After that, the fact that there was damage to the seaweed has been proven without any contradictions. The causation between the wastewater discharge of the defendant factory and the damage caused

196. Supreme Court Decision 98Da56997 Decided May 16, 2000.
197. Supreme Court Decision 73Da1253 Decided Oct. 10, 1973.
198. Supreme Court Decision 89Da1275 Decided Jul. 23, 1991.
199. Supreme Court Decision 73Da919 Decided Nov. 27, 1973.
200. Supreme Court Decision 72Da1774 Decided Dec. 10, 1974.

by the occurrence of disease in the farmed seaweed was immediately proved. Therefore, the defendant proves that ① he did not contain any causative substances that could adversely affect the growth of laver in the factory wastewater of the defendant; and ② even though a causative substance is included, if the causation cannot be denied by falsifying the fact that the seawater mixing rate is within the safe concentration range, The disadvantage should be returned to the defendant."[201]

In order to cope with the seriousness of environmental pollution, in addition to general tort liability under Article 750 of the Korean Civil Code, South Korea enacted various environmental administration laws in the 1980s and 1990s, and began to stipulate no-fault liability for compensation. For example, Article 31 of the Framework Act on Environmental Policy enacted in 1991 (current Article 44 of the Framework Act on Environmental Policy) stipulates that if any suffering is caused by environmental pollution or environmental damage, the person who has caused the environmental pollution or environmental damage shall compensate for the suffering. Thus, the liability for compensation is determined regardless of whether the person was at fault. Also, Article 23(1) of the Soil Environment Conservation Act (current Article 10-3 of the Soil Environment Conservation Act) enacted in 1995 stipulates that where any damage occurs due to soil contamination, a person who has caused the contamination shall compensate for such damage and take measures, such as purifying the contaminated soil. Therefore, it maintains the legislative attitude of no-fault responsibility. With respect to the provisions of these individual laws, no-fault responsibility for environmental pollution is stipulated. However, it has been pointed out that the risk responsibility for environmental pollution is not sufficient due to the determination of the responsible party and the applicable facilities, the content of liability and the need for limited liability in terms of amount, the relaxation of the burden of proof of causation, and the lack of regulations on the right to claim information. Meanwhile, in 2012, a series of chemical accidents, such as hydrofluoric acid leaks at a chemical plant, resulted in enormous compensation for damages, which became a social issue. Consequently, as the demand for enacting a special law to promote prompt and fair compensation for damage from environmental pollution accidents was increasing, "the Act On Liability For Environmental Damage And Relief Thereof" was enacted. Article 6 of "the Act On Liability For Environmental Damage And Relief Thereof" stipulates that where environmental damage occurs with regard to the installation and operation of a facility, a business owner of the facility shall compensate for the damage. Thus, it makes clear the no-fault liability for damages caused by environmental pollution. In addition, "the Act On Liability For Environmental Damage And Relief Thereof" provides: (1) definition of environmental pollution damage, (2) determination of responsible party and limitation of applicable facilities, (3) no-fault liability and its limitation of liability and its immunity, (4) presumption of causation and right to claim information, and (5) remedies for restoration. The right to claim damages under "the Act On Liability For Environmental Damage And Relief Thereof" is in contention of claims with the right to claim damages under the Korean Civil Code.

---

201. Supreme Court Decision 81Da558 Decided Jun. 12, 1984.

Therefore, a victim of environmental pollution may exercise the right to claim compensation for damages in accordance with tortious acts under the Korean Civil Code for damage that exceeds the limit of liability under "the Act On Liability For Environmental Damage And Relief Thereof" (Article 5(2) of the "Act On Liability For Environmental Damage And Relief Thereof").[202]

142. In order for the liability for compensation under Article 6 of "the Act On Liability For Environmental Damage And Relief Thereof" to be recognized, there shall be the following requirements: (1) occurrence of environmental damage; (2) occurrence of damage related to the installation and operation of facilities, and (3) a business owner of the facility that caused the environmental damage. First, Article 2, No. 1 of "the Act On Liability For Environmental Damage And Relief Thereof" defines the term "environmental damage" as damage (including a series of damage due to the same cause) inflicted on the life, body (including mental harm) or property of any third person by air pollution, water pollution, soil pollution, marine pollution, noise, vibration, and other causes that occur from installing and operating a facility. Through this definition, it is revealed that the responsibility for environmental damage is the responsibility of the facility. In addition, air pollution, water pollution, soil pollution, marine pollution, noise/vibration, and ground subsidence[203] are limited to the causes of environmental damage. Therefore, the scope to which no-fault responsibility is applied is limited and clarified.

In addition, the damage caused by environmental pollution refers to the damage suffered by others to personal legal interests, that is, life, body (including non-economic damage) and property due to environmental pollution. In addition to natural persons, legal entities and the state and local governments are also included in "other persons." However, the business that caused the environmental damage and the damage suffered by employees of the business operator have been excluded from the protection.

143. Facilities subject to "the Act On Liability For Environmental Damage And Relief Thereof" are limited to those stipulated in other environmental laws[204] (Article 3 of "the Act On Liability For Environmental Damage And Relief Thereof"). In other words, it is not defined as a general pollutant emission facility or a discharge facility of a certain size or larger. It is limited to facilities subject to licensing and reporting in accordance with relevant laws and regulations.

The concept of "facility" is understood in a broad sense. Thus, it includes equipment fixed to a place of business, warehouse, or land closely related to the installation and operation of the facility and includes machines, devices, vehicles, technical equipment, and accessory equipment that can be moved to new locations.

---

202. For an overview of the contents of "the Act On Liability For Environmental Damage And Relief Thereof," *see* Cho, Hong-shik, *The Commentary of Korean Civil Code—Law of Obligations (8)*, 81; Ahn Kyung-hee, *Analysis of the main contents of "the Act On Liability For Environmental Damage And Relief Thereof,"* Civil Case Study [XXXIX], 973, 2017.

203. Article 2 of Enforcement Decree Of The Act On Liability For Environmental Damage And Relief Thereof.

204. For example, facilities subject to soil pollution control as stipulated by the Soil Environment Conservation Act and air pollutant discharge facilities under the Clean Air Conservation Act.

This definition reflects the reality that environmental damage is not only directly related to the installation and operation of the facility itself but also caused by, for example, transport or loading of toxic substances.[205]

The subject of liability for compensation for environmental damage is the operator of the above facilities. "Business operator" means the owner, installer, or operator who has actual control over the relevant facility. Through the expression "actual control over the relevant facility," not only the person who legally owns the facility but also the person who has de facto control over the facility is included in the subject of liability for compensation. Regarding the concept of a business operator, it is pointed out that the meaning of "actual" is ambiguous, and if the owners, installers, and operators do not match each other, it causes difficulties in determining the subject of liability.[206] "The Act On Liability For Environmental Damage And Relief Thereof" stipulates that where at least two business owners have caused environmental damage and it is impracticable to identify which business owner is liable for the environmental damage, such business owners jointly and severally compensate for such environmental damage. (Article 10 of "The Act On Liability For Environmental Damage And Relief Thereof"). Where a person who ordered the work has contracted out the installation and operation of a facility, he or she shall be bound to manage and supervise a contractor (including a subcontractor) (Article 12 of "The Act On Liability For Environmental Damage And Relief Thereof").

144. The liability of the business operator under Article 6 of "The Act On Liability For Environmental Damage And Relief Thereof" is no-fault liability. Thus, the risk responsibility of facility owners is institutionalized. Therefore, the liability for compensation under "the Act On Liability For Environmental Damage And Relief Thereof" is different from the general tort liability under the Korean Civil Code when the facility is concerned with causing environmental damage. In this regard, it does not ask whether there is negligence regarding the illegality of the pollution and the possibility of foreseeability and preventing environmental pollution.

However, if the environmental pollution damage is caused by war, civil war, riot, natural disaster, or other force majeure, the business operator is exempted from liability for compensation. The meaning of force majeure is strictly interpreted, considering the nature of strict liability under "The Act On Liability For Environmental Damage And Relief Thereof." When a facility operator is expected to take preventive measures in preparation for natural disasters, failure to do so results in a combination of defects in installation and management. In this case, business owners are not exempted from liability for compensation. Where environmental damage occurs due to a situation that occurred before the operation of a facility was suspended, a business owner who operated the facility shall make compensation (Article 6(2) of "The Act On Liability For Environmental Damage And Relief Thereof").

205. *See* Cho, Hong-shik, *The Commentary of Korean Civil Code—Law of Obligations (8)*, 64–65.

206. For example, in the case of leasing or consignment management of a facility with a risk of inducing environmental pollution, the question arises as to who has de facto control over the facility among the lessor and lessee, the consigned owner and the consigned manager.

145. The liability for damages under "The Act On Liability For Environmental Damage And Relief Thereof" is strict liability. However, it requires the causation that environmental damage occurred due to the installation and operation of the facility. "The Act On Liability For Environmental Damage And Relief Thereof" stipulates the following presumptive provisions to ease the burden on victims of proving the causation.

Article 9 (Presumption of Causal Relationship):

(1) Where it is highly probable to believe that a facility has caused environmental damage exists, such environmental damage is presumed to have occurred from the facility.
(2) Whether sufficient probability referred to in paragraph (1) exists shall be determined in consideration of the operation process of a facility, equipment in use, types and concentration of input or discharged materials, weather conditions, when and where damage has occurred, status of damage, circumstances affecting the occurrence of damage, etc.
(3) Where a business owner proves that environmental damage has occurred due to other reasons, or that he/she has fulfilled the responsibilities under Article 4 (3), such as that he/she has observed all provisions of Acts and subordinate statutes governing the environment and safety, and all terms and conditions of authorization and permission related to the cause of occurrence of the environmental damage prescribed by Presidential Decree, and he/she has endeavored to prevent environmental damage, etc., he/she shall be exempt from presumption under paragraph (1).

It has been understood that the presumption of causation is influenced by the rule of alleviated causation (so-called probability theory) and by Article 6 of the German Environmental Responsibility Act. However, Article 9(3) of "the Act On Liability For Environmental Damage And Relief Thereof" stipulates that the reason for excluding the application of the presumptive regulations is that the business operator has operated legally through compliance with laws and regulations and preventive efforts. In this regard, a critical opinion is also presented that it is against the legislative purpose of "the Act On Liability For Environmental Damage And Relief Thereof," which is to alleviate the difficulty of the burden of proof for the victims.[207] "The Act On Liability For Environmental Damage And Relief Thereof" stipulates in detail the right to request that the victim may request a business owner of the relevant facility to provide information in detail (Article 15 of "the Act On Liability For Environmental Damage And Relief Thereof").

146. "The Act On Liability For Environmental Damage And Relief Thereof" stipulates no-fault responsibility of the facility owner for causing environmental

207. For an overview of the contents of "the Act On Liability For Environmental Damage And Relief Thereof," *see* Cho, Hong-shik, *The Commentary of Korean Civil Code—Law of Obligations (8)*, 70. On the other hand, there is the positive opinion, because this approach encourages business operators to legally manage their facilities. *See* Ahn Kyung Hee, *Analysis of the main contents of "the Act On Liability For Environmental Damage And Relief Thereof,"* Civil Case Study [XXXIX], 993, 2017.

damage. However, by setting the limit of liability for compensation, this Act seeks to achieve a balanced position between the victim and the business operator (Article 7 of "the Act On Liability For Environmental Damage And Relief Thereof"). The liability cap of a business owner for compensation for environmental damage shall be prescribed by Presidential Decree within a maximum of KRW 200 billion, based upon the scale of the relevant facility, the result of damage to occur, etc. However, it does not apply in any of the following circumstances: (1) where environmental damage occurs due to intentional or gross negligence of the business owner; (2) where the business owner fails to observe relevant Acts and subordinate statutes, such as that he/she fails to observe safety management standards related to the installation and operation of a facility that has caused damage, he/she discharges pollutants in excess of permissible discharge limits, etc.; (3) where the business owner who has caused environmental damage fails to take adequate measures to prevent and control the environmental damage, such as prevention of spread of damage.

As for the reasons for exclusion of the limit of liability, the victim bears the burden of proof. Article 17 of "the Act On Liability For Environmental Damage And Relief Thereof" provides obligation to purchase environmental liability insurance for business operators who install and operate facilities that are at risk of causing environmental damage. In addition, where a victim fails to fully or partially receive compensation for environmental damage, the Minister of Environment may pay money for relief from environmental damage to the victim or his/her bereaved family members. The grounds are: (1) where a person who causes environmental damage is unknown, his/her existence is not obvious, or he/she is insolvent; (2) where the relief money exceeds the liability cap for compensation (Article 7 of "the Act On Liability For Environmental Damage And Relief Thereof").

147. Environmental damage shall be indemnified monetarily. However, where re-instatement is possible without incurring excess expenses compared with the amount of indemnity payments, a victim of environmental damage may request re-instatement (Article 13 of "the Act On Liability For Environmental Damage And Relief Thereof"). Where environmental damage arising from a facility simultaneously causes damage to the natural environment, a victim of the environmental damage may request re-instatement to the relevant business owner or directly reinstate the damaged part. If the victim of such environmental damage directly reinstates the damaged part, he or she may request the relevant business owner to reimburse for expenses incurred in such re-instatement (Article 14 of "the Act On Liability For Environmental Damage And Relief Thereof"). Environmental damage in "the Act On Liability For Environmental Damage And Relief Thereof" means an infringement on personal legal interests. A victim's claim for restoration includes restoration of the natural environment or natural scenery. However, in order to avoid excessive burden on business operators, "the Act On Liability For Environmental Damage And Relief Thereof" limits the content of restoration to the original state by saying "no excessive cost" or "compensation within a reasonable range." However, the natural environment or natural scenery is limited to the contents according to individual environment laws.[208] It is considered that there would be many difficulties in interpretation regarding the restoration to its original state.

208. Natural Environment Conservation Act defines the terms natural environment and natural scenery. According to Art. 2, No. 1, "natural environment" means the state of nature (including the ecosystem and natural scenery) which includes all living things under the ground, on the surface of the earth (excluding the ocean) and on the ground, and the inanimate things surrounding these. And Art. 2, No. 10 of this Act says that "natural scenery" is an area, topography and elements of nature affiliated with them that have visual or aesthetic value in terms of the natural environment, or scenery of nature where things are harmonious in a complex way.

Chapter 5. Others

§1. Strict Liability under the Civil Code

148. As mentioned before, when damage is caused to others due to defects in the installation or preservation of the structure (Article 758(1) of the Korean Civil Code), the liability for compensation borne by the owner of a structure is the only non-fault liability stipulated in the tort law of the Korean Civil Code.

149. According to Article 761(2) of the Korean Civil Code, in case of inevitably causing damage to another person in order to avert an imminent danger, victims may claim compensation for damages against the person who caused the danger by tortious acts. However, the emergency evacuator cannot be held liable for damages.[209] As introduced below, the illegality of emergency evacuation is excluded. As a result, the tortfeasor cannot be held responsible for the consequences of the harm. In that respect, it can be understandable partially. However, it is harsh to force the injured person who suffered damage from the emergency evacuation act to bear the consequences of the harm. Therefore, many South Korean scholars have proposed to stipulate no-fault liability for the injured person by emergency evacuees, as other countries have dealt with the cases.

§2. Other Provisions of Strict Liability

150. Beyond the Korean Civil Code, individual laws stipulate strict liability concerning dangerous activities. In addition to the liability provisions covered so far, we can first mention liability under the Mining Industry Act. In 1951, even before the Korean Civil Code was enacted, the Mining Industry Act already stipulated the no-fault liability of the mining rights holder for compensation without negligence or intentional negligence. When significant damages are inflicted on other persons due to the excavation of land, discharge of pit water or waste water, piling of waste stone or mineral scraps, or discharge of mine smoke for the purpose of extracting minerals, the person shall be liable to compensate for the damages (Article 75(1) of the Mining Industry Act). Compensation for damages is made in money. However, if the damaged property can be restored to its original state without requiring excessive expenses, compared with monetary compensation, the victim may demand restoration of the property to its original state. Thus, a court may, upon request by a person liable for damages, order restoration of the property to its original state in lieu of monetary compensation if deemed proper (Article 77 of the Mining Industry

209. Article 761 (Self-Defense and Act of Necessity) of the Korean Civil Code:

(1) A person who, in order to protect his own interest or that of a third person against an unlawful act of another, unavoidably causes damages to another person shall not be liable for such damages: Provided, That the injured party may claim for damages in respect of the unlawful act.
(2) The provisions of paragraph (1) shall apply mutatis mutandis where a person unavoidably caused damages to another person in order to avert an imminent danger.

Act). If a victim is partly responsible for damages, the court shall take such facts into consideration in determining the liability and the scope of compensation for the damages. The same shall apply where natural disasters or other unavoidable causes concurrently contribute to the occurrence of the damages (Article 78 of the Mining Industry Act).

151. In addition, the Nuclear Liability Act enacted in 1969 also stipulates the strict liability of nuclear operators. Article 3(1) of the Nuclear Liability Act provides that where nuclear damage is caused by the operation of a nuclear reactor, the relevant nuclear business operator shall be liable for such damage. The term "nuclear damage" means damage (including the loss of economic interests related to the use of the environment, which is caused by serious environmental damage) caused by the nuclear fission process of nuclear fuel materials, or by radiation or by the toxicity of nuclear fuel materials or materials contaminated thereby, and the following expenses: (a) expenses for measures taken or to be taken to recover from serious environmental damage to the original state according to plans formulated under relevant Acts and (b) expenses for measures for preventing disasters taken according to measures plans formulated under relevant Acts to mitigate or minimize damage or expenses caused by the outbreak of nuclear incidents or to prevent or minimize damage or expenses caused by grave and imminent danger which may cause a nuclear incident. On the other hand, the Nuclear Liability Act only mentions "when nuclear damage occurs due to armed conflict between nations, hostility, civil war, or rebellion" as the reason for exclusion of no-fault liability. Thus, the Nuclear Liability Act defines force majeure reasons narrowly because other individual laws on strict liability are subject to natural disasters and other force majeure reasons. A nuclear business operator shall assume liability for nuclear damage within the limit of a calculation unit of 300 million for each nuclear incident. However, no limitation of liabilities for damage shall apply where a nuclear business operator causes nuclear damage intentionally, or by reckless conduct or by willful blindness to the likelihood of the damage (Article 3-2 of the Nuclear Liability Act).

Nuclear business operators are obliged to subscribe to a nuclear liability insurance contract for business operations.

152. Regarding the introduction of strict liability by individual legislation, it is proposed to introduce strict liability in the pharmaceutical and genetic engineering fields according to the recent legislative influence of Germany and other countries.[210] Also, in the course of discussing the revision of the Korean Civil Code, it has been proposed to put general provisions on strict liability within the Korean Civil Code. However, it has not yet been accepted.[211]

210. Shin, Yu-Chul, *Development of Life Sciences and Civil Liability*, The Journal of Korean Civil Law No. 22, pp. 13 et seq., 2002.

211. Kim, Sang-Joong, *Current Status of Risk Responsibilities and Legislative Discussion in Korea*, The Journal of Korean Civil Law No. 57, pp. 163 et seq., 2011.

Part IV. Defenses and Exception Clauses

Chapter 1. Limitation of Action

153. Article 766 of the Korean Civil Code stipulates the time to exercise the right to claim compensation for tortious acts. According to this provision, the right to claim for damages resulting from an unlawful act shall lapse by prescription if not exercised within three years commencing from the date on which the injured party or his/her legal representative becomes aware of such damage and of the identity of the person who caused it (Article 766(1) of the Korean Civil Code). However, the provisions of paragraph (1) also apply if ten years have elapsed from the time when the unlawful act was committed. Article 766(3) was newly added in October 2020. It provides that where a minor suffers from sexual violence, sexual molestation, sexual harassment, or other sexual infringement, the extinctive prescription of the right to claim compensation for damages shall not proceed until such minor attains the majority. The statute of limitations for a general claim is ten years regardless of whether the creditor's subjective perception of the right to arise (Article 162(1) of the Korean Civil Code). However, the statute of limitations for tort claims is a relative period of three years from the date the victim became aware of the damage and the tortfeasor. In addition, the absolute period of ten years from the date of the tortious act regardless of the subjective perception of the victim. As for the reason for the short-term extinctive prescription of three years, according to the theory of many South Korean scholars, it becomes difficult to prove the tort requirements or to calculate the amount of damage after a long period of time. Also, it suggests that the injured party's feelings will subside over time.

154. The starting point of the three-year prescription period under Article 766(1) of the Korean Civil Code is the date the victim or his/her legal representative became aware of the damage and the tortfeasor. "The date of knowing the damage and the tortfeasor" means "the fact that there is the occurrence of the damage, the existence of a tortious act, and an adequate causation between the damage and the tortious act." It refers to the time when realistic and concrete recognition of the tortious act is required. Therefore, even if it is known that the damage has occurred, the prescription does not proceed if it is not known that the inflicted act is a tortious act. In addition, it must be recognized that the victim had the mental ability or intelligence to recognize realistically and concretely that the damage occurred and that the damage was caused by the tortious act of the tortfeasor. Otherwise, even after the accident occurred, even if the victim had heard about the accident, it would not be possible to say that he or she knew the damage and the tortfeasor. Therefore, this short-term extinction prescription does not proceed.[212]

In a case where new damage that could not have been foreseen at the time of the tort occurs, such as aftereffects from an injury, or the damage expands unexpectedly, it can be considered that the newly occurred or expanded damage was known when such a cause becomes clear. Therefore, the statute of limitations expires at that point.[213] Furthermore, if the tort is not a one-time but continuous (e.g., illegal occupation, obstruction of sunlight), it is considered that damages are caused by new torts every day. Therefore, each day, the extinctive prescription proceeds separately from the day on which each damage caused by the new tort is known. Regarding the time when the victim or his/her legal representative became aware of the damage and the tortfeasor, the person obligated to compensate, claiming the completion of the short-term prescription shall prove it.

However, the time when the unlawful act was committed, which is the starting point of the ten-year absolute statute of limitations, is not the day on which the infringement occurred. This is the time when it can be seen that the damage that should have been said to have existed only potentially state has been realized due to the tortious act. In other words, it means when damage has occurred objectively and specifically. Therefore, for example, the South Korean Supreme Court held as follows. If the incubation period of infection is long or it is difficult to predict to what stage the disease will progress at the time of infection, there may be damages caused by the onset of symptoms or disease progression in addition to the damage caused by the infection itself. Therefore, the Supreme Court decided that such damage occurred realistically at the time the symptoms appeared, or the disease progressed, when the incubation period of infection is long, or when it is difficult to predict what stage the disease will progress to at the time of infection. In addition to the damage caused by the infection itself, there may be damage caused by the onset of symptoms or the progression of the disease. Therefore, it was judged that such damage can be regarded as realistically occurring at the time when symptoms appear or the disease progresses.

155. Article 766 of the Korean Civil Code on the extinctive prescription of the right to claim for damages due to torts is applied *mutatis mutandis* to the right to claim damages due to an automobile accident as stipulated by individual laws (Article 4 of the Guarantee of Automobile Accident Compensation Act). However, individual laws on strict liability set a separate statute of limitations on the victim's right to claim damages (e.g., Article 7 of the Product Liability Act, Article 13-2 of the Nuclear Liability Act).

156. Articles 168 and 179 of the Korean Civil Code provide for the causes of interrupting extinctive prescription and suspension of prescription. Therefore, the causes interrupting extinctive prescription and suspension of prescription of claims for damages due to torts are also governed by Articles 168 and 179 of the Korean

212. Supreme Court Decision 94Da30263 Decided Feb. 10, 1995.
213. Supreme Court Decision 98Da30285 Decided Mar. 23, 1999.

Civil Code. According to Article 168 of the Korean Civil Code, extinctive prescription is interrupted in any of the following cases: demand; attachment, provisional attachment or provisional disposition; acknowledgment. A peremptory notice shall have no effect of interrupting prescription unless a demand by judicial proceedings, intervention in bankruptcy proceedings, a summons for compromise or a voluntary appearance for the same purpose, an attachment, a provisional attachment or a provisional disposition is taken within six months (Article 174 of the Korean Civil Code). Where it is impossible to interrupt extinctive prescription because of a natural calamity or any other accidents, prescription shall not become complete for a period of one month from the time when such obstacle ceases to exist. (Article 182 of the Korean Civil Code).

157. The fact that the extinctive prescription period for the right to claim compensation for tortious acts has expired is not a matter for the court to investigate ex officio. Therefore, the defendant obligated to indemnify the defendant must assert and prove it as a defense. After the statute of limitations expires, the debtor does not have a legal obligation to pay it back. However, if it has been paid, the creditor may not demand the return of it.

Chapter 2. Grounds of Justification

§1. CONSENT

158. The consent of the victim precludes the establishment of a tort. For example, it is not illegal for a doctor to infringe on a patient's body for the purpose of examining or treating a disease with the patient's consent. Therefore, it does not constitute a tortious act. The Korean Civil Code does not stipulate the consent of the victim as a ground for exclusion of illegality. However, theories of Korean scholars and courts understand that the victim's consent can exclude illegality within a reasonable range. This is because, according to the principle of private autonomy, one's legal interests are entrusted to one's own free disposition. Article 24 of the Korean Criminal Code stipulates that an act which infringes a legal interest with the consent of a person who is authorized to dispose of such interest shall not be punishable.

159. As a ground for exclusion of illegality, the victim's consent must be based on his or her free will. In addition, the victim must have the mental capacity to fully understand the meaning and content of the damage caused. Therefore, even in a case in which the victim's consent is obtained, if the tortious act is performed for a different purpose or method than expected at the time of consent, exceeding the scope of consent, its illegality cannot be excluded. For example, the South Korean Supreme court case held as follows. "The victim consented to broadcasting about the side effects of her medical operation on condition that people would not be able to recognize her. At the time of the broadcast, the figure of the victim was treated as a shadow. However, the outline of the profile appeared in the shadows. Appropriate measures of broadcasting technology, such as voice modulation, were not taken. As a result, the identity of the victim was exposed to the people around her. In this case, the victim's privacy was unfairly disclosed in a different way than expected at the time of consent, exceeding the scope of consent of the victim."[214] Furthermore, the consent of the victim must not violate good morals or other social order. Requests for aiding suicide, such as disposing of life or accepting serious bodily injury, are against public order and morals, and the illegality of the tortious act is not excluded.

160. A victim's consent is treated similarly to a declaration of intention. Therefore, it is possible to consent not only in an explicit form but also in an implicit one. For example, when a person participating in a sports game with a high risk of injury inherent in the competition because it often involves physical contact is at a considerable risk within the range that can be foreseen, there is an implied consent in the sense of accepting this and attending the game.[215]

In addition, the victim must have his or her mental ability when consenting. In the case of being unable to effectuate the juristic act of the contract by oneself, such as a minor, if he or she has the ability to understand the meaning and extent of the

214. Supreme Court Decision 96Da11327 Decided Sep. 4, 1998.
215. Supreme Court Decision 2011Da66849, 66856 Decided Dec. 8, 2011.

infringement, the minor can consent. However, in the case of medical practice, the victim's consent has frequently been a problem. Although a minor has the ability to determine, parental consent is also considered necessary.

§2. Necessity

161. In case of unavoidably causing damage to another person in order to avert an imminent danger, Article 761(2) of the Korean Civil Code excludes the illegality of the offense and does not recognize responsibility for the tortious act. Unlike self-defense, which will be introduced below, act of necessity is an act of evacuation against violations that are not illegal. Act of necessity is caused not only by the actions of others but also by imminent danger caused by other people's goods or natural phenomena such as natural disasters.

In order for act of necessity to be recognized, there are three factors: (1) to protect the interests of oneself or a third party; (2) to protect the current imminent violation; (3) it must be an unavoidable act. However, it is not act of necessity when the imminent danger is caused by the tortfeasor's own intention or negligence. In addition, there must be no room for national relief because of an imminent danger, and there must be no other evacuation method other than harming the interests of others to avoid the imminent danger.

Furthermore, to determine whether to exclude the illegality of harmful acts as act of necessity, it should be considered whether social relevance is recognized between the interests to be protected from the imminent danger and the interests violated in order to avoid the danger.

Therefore, in the case of inflicting serious injury on another person in order to avoid harm to minor property and legal interests, the illegality of act of necessity is not excluded. The same applies to the case in which a person causes damage to another person as act of necessity in misunderstanding, although there is not an imminent danger.

162. The act of necessity excludes illegality. Therefore, a person who causes damage to another person in order to avert an imminent danger is not responsible for compensating for the damage to the victim (Article 761(2) of the Korean Civil Code). If the danger was caused by a tortious act (by a person other than the evacuee), the victim of the act of necessity may claim compensation for damages against the person who illegally caused the imminent danger. For the legislatively aspect, to protect victims of act of necessity beyond the cases of danger caused illegally, there have been arguments that the victim should be able to claim substantial compensation from the evacuee, considering the cause of the danger, the details of the evacuation, and the nature and extent of the damage.

§3. Self-Help and Self-Defense

163. The Korean Civil Code does not have a general provision regarding self-help. However, in order to protect the right to possession, which is considered a type of property right, Article 209 of the Korean Civil Code stipulates self-help only in the case of unjustly depriving the possessor of his or her rightful possession.[216] The question of whether self-help can be accepted in other cases has been controversial. The majority position of South Korean scholars have understood that the Korean Civil Code provides self-help only in the case of unjustly depriving the possessor of his or her rightful possession. Thus, it does not recognize self-help in other cases.

Meanwhile, Article 23 of the Korean Criminal Code Act stipulates that it excludes the punitive nature of self-help actions related to the preservation of claims. In regard to this, self-help is recognized as one of the grounds for exclusion of civil illegality. However, self-help, like act of necessity, must be an imminent and unavoidable case where it is impossible to wait for relief according to the procedure stipulated by the law. In addition, the means used for self-help must be recognized as necessary and appropriate for remedies.

164. Article 761(1) of the Korean Civil Code provides that a person who, in order to protect his own interest or that of a third person against an unlawful act of another, unavoidably causes damages to another person shall not be liable for such damages. This is self-defense and its illegality is excluded. The self-defense provision shows that a person does not have to yield to illegality. Self-defense requires that danger be caused by the tortious acts of others. A person who has acted illegally does not have to have intention or negligence and responsible capacity.

However, act of necessity may be a problem for violations caused by animals, inanimate objects, and natural disasters other than human actions. However, it is not subject to self-defense.

Also, if it is an act to defend the interests of oneself or a third party, it does not have to be about tortfeasors who caused the danger. Defensive actions against third parties are also permitted.

Furthermore, in the case of self-defense, as in the case of act of necessity, there should be no suitable method other than the act of causing harm because the infringement is imminent. A reasonable balance between the legal interests to be defended and the infringed legal interests must be recognized. In the case of excessive defense in which a reasonable balance between such protection and infringement interests is not recognized, and in the case in which although the requirements for self-defense were not objectively given, the actor subjectively misunderstood that the defense act was necessary and self-defense is not recognized.

165. There is no illegality in the actions of a self-defender. Accordingly, the self-defense party is not liable for compensation to the victims suffered through self-defense. However, if self-defense is an imputation type, which is in the case of

216. Article 209 (Self-help):

(1) A possessor may defend, with his own force, his possession against those acts unjustly depriving him of his rightful possession or disturbing it.
(2) If the possessor of an immovable has been deprived of possession thereof, the possessor may recapture it by evicting the assailant immediately after the deprivation; and if it is a movable, the possessor may recapture from the assailant, on the spot or in pursuit, the article in question.

inflicting damage to a third party other than the torts in order to avoid the tortious act inflicted upon him or her, injured parties may claim compensation for damages against the person who caused the unlawful danger. In this case, the tortfeasor (who caused legitimate defense) must have intention or negligent and responsible capacity for his or her tortious act.

§4. Others

166. The grounds for exclusion of illegality from civil liability are found not only in the Korean Civil Code but also in the case of victim consent and self-help. The legal basis is sought in the Korean Criminal Code. Article 20 of the Korean Criminal Code provides that an act which is conducted in accordance with Acts and subordinate statutes, or in pursuance of accepted business practices, or other action which does not violate the social rules shall not be punishable. From a civil point of view, a justifiable act is considered a reason for exclusion of illegality if it has social validity. For example, any person may arrest a flagrant offender without a warrant as a justifiable act (Article 212 of the Korean Criminal Procedure Act). In addition, industrial actions by workers who have justification under the Labor Law (Articles 3 and 4 of the Trade Union and Labor Relations Adjustment Act) fall into this category.

167. Finally, when the violation of personality rights such as invasion of privacy or defamation occurred in the process of realizing the public's right to know or public interest, or in the process of using neighboring land, if there is an obstruction to life to the extent that it normally accompanies the use of the land, such acts of infringement of interests are not recognized as illegal.

168. The defense of contributory negligence is stipulated in Article 396 of the Korean Civil Code. Article 396 of the Korean Civil Code stipulates contributory negligence from liability for breach of contract, which is applied *mutatis mutandis* to tort liability (Article 763 of the Korean Civil Code). According to it, if the victim is at fault for the occurrence or expansion of damage caused by torts, this must be taken into account when determining whether or not to be liable for damages or the amount of compensation.[217] The grounds for acknowledging contributory negligence are generally based on the viewpoint of fairness. In other words, imputing damage caused by one's own negligence to others is contrary to the purpose of the damage compensation law concerning equitable sharing of damages. Therefore, the damage caused by his or her own negligence should be borne by the victim himself or herself. Article 396 of the Korean Civil Code provides that if there has been any

217. Regarding the term of contributory negligence, Korean scholars have argued that the term of contributory negligence is not appropriate. For this reason, it is also referred to as joint negligence or competition of negligence. This is understood in the same meaning as comparative negligence of the English and American law.

negligence on the part of the obligee in regard to the nonperformance of the obligation, the court shall take it into account in determining the liability for and assessing the amount of the damages. Therefore, not only can the amount of compensation be reduced by comparing the negligence of the victim and the tortfeasor, but also the responsibility of the tortfeasor can be denied if the negligence of the victim is serious.

169. According to the majority theory of South Korean scholars and case laws, the victim's negligence for recognition of contributory negligence is different from negligence for torts or breach of contract. Therefore, it is understood as weak carelessness or simple carelessness required in the communal life of society. The Supreme Court of Korea ruled as follows: "The purpose of the contributory negligence stipulated in articles 763 and 396 of the Korean Civil Code is different from that of making the torts actively liable for damages. Therefore, when the victim does not fulfill the precautions required by the law of good faith in living a social life, in determining the liability of the tortfeasor for damages and the amount of damages to be compensated, it is intended to take into account the negligence of the victim regarding the occurrence of damage, in accordance with the principle of fairness, which is the guiding principle of the damage compensation law. Therefore, when the victim violates the duty of care in the strict sense required for the establishment of a tortious act, and when the damage is caused and expanded due to simple negligence, the victim is at fault. Therefore, contributory negligence may work in these cases."[218]

The negligence of contributory negligence is understood differently from negligence for the recognition of tort or breach of contract. According to this view, the responsibility competency of the victim (Articles 753 and 754 of the Korean Civil Code) is not required for the recognition of contributory negligence. However, the victim must have the determination capacity to pay the necessary attention to avoid the occurrence of damage. Therefore, it is held that a young child, for example, about 6 years old, does not have sufficient ability to recognize and avoid danger by means of transportation. Therefore, the negligence necessary for contributory negligence was not recognized in this case.[219]

170. Article 396 of the Korean Civil Code simply mentions the term "creditor." In other words, in the case of torts, it only refers to the negligence of the "injured party." However, in accordance with the purpose of contributory negligence of equitable sharing of damages, the negligence of a third party other than the victim is also taken into account in determining whether or not to be liable for damage compensation. For example, in relation to the lessee's breach of contact liability for the preservation of the leased object to the lessor, the negligence of the employee of the lessee may be recognized as a cause for contributory negligence.[220] In addition, if the person responsible for supervision of an incompetent person is at fault, the negligence of the person responsible for supervision may be taken into account as the

218. Supreme Court Decision 92Da6112 Decided May 12, 1992.
219. Supreme Court Decision 74Da1882 Decided Dec. 24, 1974.
220. Supreme Court Decision 96Da30113 Decided Oct. 25, 1996.

cause of contributory negligence of the victim. Furthermore, the South Korean Supreme Court has expanded the scope of a third party that can be taken into account as the victim's negligence: "to those who are in an integral relationship in terms of identity or life" with the victim.

For example, in a claim for damages from a sister caused by an accident while riding on the back seat of a motorcycle that her brother was driving, contributory negligence was also recognized for her brother's driving negligence.[221]

171. The victim's negligence, which is taken into account as a cause of contributory negligence, refers to the victim's carelessness. In this case, the victim's negligence includes not only the occurrence of the damage but also the expansion of the damage after the tortious act.

In accordance with the equitable sharing of damages, in addition to the victim's carelessness, when the victim's predisposition, such as the victim's diathesis, past medical history, and other physical conditions, is combined with the tortfeasor's actions to increase the occurrence of damage to the victim, the South Korean Supreme Court has applied the principle of contributory negligence by analogy.[222] Some South Korean scholars have criticized this approach of the Supreme Court. However, the Supreme Court has applied this principle. For example, in a case in which a newborn baby died because it was deemed that there was no possibility of surviving a preterm low-weight twin and did not take necessary medical measures, the amount of damage was reduced by taking into account the extent to which the poor physical predisposition of newborns contributed to the death while regarding the loss of lost income up to the average life expectancy.[223] For the recognition of contributory negligence, there must be a causation between the negligence of the victim and the damage. However, it does not require the degree of adequate causation necessary for the establishment of tort liability. However, it is understood that it is sufficient if there is a relevance between the negligence of the victim and the damage. The South Korean Supreme Court dealt with a case in which while a civilian was riding in a military vehicle without due process and without justifiable reasons, an accident occurred,[224] and with a case in which a person was riding with a friend after drinking with him.[225] The Supreme Court considered the victim's behavior to be a factor in contributory negligence.

172. Contributory negligence applies to contractual or tortious damages liability that requires the liability of the debtor or tortfeasor. In principle, contributory negligence is recognized not only when the debtor or tortfeasor is negligent but also when the negligence of the creditor or victim competes with the intentional breach of contract or illegal activity of the debtor or tortfeasor. However, in the case of an intentional tortious act such as fraud, embezzlement, or breach of trust, using the

221. Supreme Court Decision 72Da2082 Decided Sep. 25, 1973.
222. Supreme Court Decision 98Da50586 Decided Jan. 21, 2000.
223. Supreme Court Decision 94Da29218 Decided Apr. 14, 1995.
224. Supreme Court Decision 67Da334 Decided May 23, 1967.
225. Supreme Court Decision 91Da39306 Decided Jan. 21, 1992.

negligence of the victim, if contributory negligence is applicable, the tortfeasor ultimately has the profits from his or her tortious act, which goes against fairness. Therefore, in these cases, contributory negligence is exceptionally not allowed.[226] Contributory negligence also applies to no-fault liability without questioning whether the tortfeasor was at fault. For example, according to Article 758 of the Korean Civil Code, the owner of a structure bears strict liability for damage caused by defects in installation or preservation of the structure.[227] Contributory negligence is recognized if the victim is also at fault in the occurrence or expansion of the damage. In the case of liability for damage due to mine damage under Article 75 of the Mining Industry Act, which is strict liability, it is stipulated that if there is a cause for which the victim is responsible for the occurrence of the damage, it should be considered when determining the liability and scope of the compensation (Article 78 of the Mining Industry Act).

226. Supreme Court Decision 2006Da16758, 16765 Decided Oct. 25, 2007.
227. Supreme Court Decision 91Da29767 Decided Dec. 24, 1991.

Chapter 3. Exemption Clauses

173. Immunity agreement, which is an agreement between the parties on the conditions or content of liability for damages, is generally dealt with in the area of contract liability. In principle, the immunity agreement of the parties regarding contract liability does not apply to tort liability in accordance with the majority theory of contention of claims. In South Korean precedent, it is said that the liability for breach of contract under the contract of carriage and liability for damages due to tort coexist. Therefore, the South Korean Supreme Court has held that the express or implied agreement to extend the tort liability is required in order to be applied to tort liability, as the special clause in the contract of carriage does not naturally apply to tort liability.[228] As an exception to this, in the case of carriage by sea, the South Korean Supreme Court held that the terms and conditions of immunity written on the bill of lading by the carriage carrier would be applied to tort liability without a separate agreement other than liability for breach of contract.[229] However, with the amendment of the Korean Commercial Code in 1991, a provision was newly established that the provisions on the contract liability of the sea carrier also apply to the carrier's liability for tortious acts. In the case of air transportation, the expanded application of liability to tort liability was newly established with the revision of the Korean Commercial Code in 2011.

Immunity agreements allowed in principle according to the principle of private autonomy are possible only if they do not violate social order. The Korean Supreme Court also ruled as follows: "An agreement between the tortfeasor and the victim to exempt or limit the tort liability for the infringement of property rights due to intention or gross negligence in advance is an act against social order and is invalid." When the indemnity agreement is not in the form of individual agreements between the parties but in the form of terms and conditions for use in repeated transactions with multiple parties, the Act on the Regulation of Terms and Conditions deals with these cases. Article 7 of the Act on the Regulation of Terms and Conditions provides that a clause in terms and conditions concerning the liability of contracting parties that falls under any of the following subparagraphs shall be null and void. The Act says that a clause which exempts a businessperson from liability for intentional or gross negligence on the part of the businessperson is void. The Act also deals with a clause which limits, without a substantial reason, the extent of indemnification payable by a businessperson or which passes a risk to be borne by a businessperson to a customer and a clause which, without a substantial reason, excludes or limits the warranty liability of a businessperson, or tightens requirements of customers to exercise the rights under warranty thereof as null and void.

228. Supreme Court Decision 2001Da58269 Decided Jul. 22, 2004.

229. Supreme Court Decision *en banc* 82DaKa1533 Decided Mar. 22, 1983.

Part V. Causality

174. In order to be held liable for damages caused by torts, there must be a causation between the tortfeasor's actions and the damage. Article 750 of the Korean Civil Code clarifies this, stipulating, "Any person who causes losses to or inflicts injuries on another person by an unlawful act, intentionally or negligently, shall be bound to make compensation for damages arising therefrom." Even in the cases of product liability and environmental pollution damage, regardless of negligence, expressions such as "damage to the life, body, or property caused by a defect in the product" (Article 3(1) of the Product Liability Act), or "damage inflicted on the life, body or property of any third person by air pollution, ... and other causes that occur from installing and operating a facility show this" (Article 2 No. 1. of Act On Liability For Environmental Damage And Relief Thereof).

The Korean Civil Code does not specifically provide for the essential requirement for liability for damages, that is, the existence of a causation between the tortfeasor's actions and the damage. Therefore, the meaning and specific content of the causation have been determined by theories and precedents. The theories of causation in South Korea have been influenced by German theories in the civil law area.

In the case where a causation between the tortfeasor's actions and the occurrence of damage is established, there must be a cause and effect between the tortfeasor's tortious act and the victim's damage. In addition, among the damages continuously occurring to the victim, the causation is divided into causality to determine the extent of the damages regarding the extent to which the tortfeasor is to compensate the victim. In addition, a causation is needed regarding the extent to which the tortfeasor is to compensate for the damages that occur continuously to the victim. Therefore, there are two causations. The former causal relation is the causation necessary to establish responsibility (causation for responsibility establishment). The latter causal relationship is a causation for determining the scope of damages (causation for responsibility satisfaction).[230] Recent South Korean literatures have strictly divided causation for responsibility establishment and causation for responsibility satisfaction. In the latter case, normative determinations are made according to adequate causation. However, it is argued that it is sufficient to make a factual determination according to the "but-for" test.

Normative determinations on whether to establish responsibility are already being made based on the requirements of illegality and intention or negligence. Therefore, a causation would be sufficient as it is determined by facts. According to this

230. In this respect, these two causations are very similar to cause in fact and proximate causation in American and English Tort Law.

position, the causation of establishment of responsibility is sufficient only as a conditional causation, that is, a relationship that a certain result would not have occurred without a certain cause (*conditio sine qua non*).

However, the traditional theories and South Korean courts have not strictly distinguished the causation for responsibility establishment from the causation for responsibility satisfaction. Thus, they have determined the adequate causation. The adequate causation means that a relationship that normally causes a certain subsequent result while considering objectively antecedent facts. The South Korean Supreme Court held, "In order to determine the presence or absence of an adequate causation, taking into account the overall factors: the probability of the occurrence of a general outcome; protection objectives laws and regulations of conduct that impose a duty of care; the nature of the infringement and the nature of the infringed interest and the extent of the damage."[231] Determination of a causation is related to whether such responsibility is established. For example, when a public official violates his or her duties and causes damage to the victim, whether the victim's damage can be attributed to the violation of duty is considered important in the type of case in question.

175. When multiple acts or circumstances are involved in the occurrence of damage, the determination of causation and attribution of responsibility becomes problematic. In South Korea, a case of several harmful acts, a case in which the tortfeasor and natural force compete, and a case in which the tortious act and the victim's prior medical history are in competition have mainly been treated as contention of causes. First, in the case where the harm caused by multiple persons competes to cause damage, the result of damage may occur even if any one of them did not act. Therefore, according to this conditional causation, it is difficult to recognize a causation between each act and damage.

In this regard, Article 760(1) of the Korean Civil Code provides that if two or more persons have, by their joint unlawful acts, caused damages to another, they shall be jointly and severally liable to make compensation for such damages. The majority theory and the South Korean court interpret the meaning of "joint" in the provision broadly. Thus, it is not limited to cases where multiple actors collude to commit a tortious act (so-called subjective joint). Therefore, joint torts are recognized even when each independent act is related to each other in time and place and causes a harm (so-called objective joint). In this case, the persons involved are liable for damage in a relationship of (imperfect) joint and several obligations. South Korean courts have recognized responsibility for all damages in relation to the victim, even if the degree of tortious act by one tortfeasor is insignificant compared to other tortfeasors when "joint" is provided.[232] In addition, Article 760(3) of the

231. Supreme Court Decision 91Da43466 Decided Feb. 12, 1993; Supreme Court Decision 2002Da62678 Decided Feb. 14, 2003; Supreme Court Decision 2005Da21821 Decided Jul. 13, 2007; Supreme Court Decision 2006Da81325 Decided Jul. 23, 2009.

232. Even if there is no subjective joint will, South Korean courts have applied joint tort liability. Therefore, it has included the risk of excessively expanding the responsibilities of those involved. Accordingly, courts and theories have been attempting to reduce responsibility through the denial of "joint" in specific cases and the degree of "contributory negligence" by the victim to each actor.

Korean Civil Code stipulates the responsibility to compensate the victim for damage, treating the instigators and accessories as joint tortfeasors. Furthermore, Article 760(2) of the Korean Civil Code provides that if it is impossible to ascertain which of the participants, albeit not joint, has caused the damages, they are treated as joint tortfeasors. For example, A and B accidentally fired guns in the same direction while hunting and injured the victim. This is an alternative causal case where it is not possible to know whether the victim was injured by a bullet fired from whose gun. Thus, a provision called "illegal act of unknown tortfeasor" has been established, requiring each tortfeasor to bear the full liability for damages. The purpose of this provision is to shift the burden of proving the causation between the tortious act and the occurrence of damage to the tortfeasor for the protection of the victim. Therefore, in order to avoid liability, the tortfeasor must prove that there is no causation between his act and the damage.

Second, when the contention between the tortfeasor and the natural force is an issue, if the tortious act is the cause of the damage, the tortfeasor's liability for damages is recognized even though it competes with natural force. In this case, the liability for compensation may be reduced according to the involvement of natural force. However, when the duty of care borne by the tortfeasor includes the duty to foresee and avoid the contribution of natural forces to the occurrence of damage, the tortfeasor's liability for compensation is not reduced by reason of the contribution of natural force.[233]

Third, if the victim's previous medical history competes with the tortious act and contributes to the expansion of damage, the Supreme Court of South Korea reduces liability for compensation by denying the causation between the tortious act and the result of the damage to the extent that the victim's previous medical history contributed to the overall injury, considering the purport of equitable sharing of damages.[234]

176. As a special topic of causation, superseding or hypothetical causation has been discussed.

A hypothetical causation is a case when a causation between an action and the occurrence of damage is recognized, but the same result can occur with another action that precedes it or another action that follows. This is the case, for example, when a victim who died in a traffic accident already drank a pesticide that exceeded the lethal dose just before the accident occurred.[235] In this case, according to the conditional causation theory, no causation is recognized for the occurrence of damage in both acts. However, such a view is unfair. Accordingly, the liability for compensation is generally recognized for the causative act involved in the occurrence of the damage.[236] As such a hypothetical causation, whether or not to defend a legitimate substitute act by the tortfeasor is also being discussed. In this case, it is established that the tortious act of the tortfeasor caused the damage. However, the

233. Supreme Court Decision 2001Da734 Decided Jun. 27, 2003.
234. Supreme Court Decision 2004Da47734 Decided Nov. 26, 2004.
235. Supreme Court Decision 94Da47179 Decided Feb. 14, 1995.
236. For regarding the contention of the tortious acts, *see* Lee, Yeon-gap, *The Commentary of Korean Civil Code—Law of Obligations (6)*, 243–245, 2022.

question is whether the tortfeasor can be exempted from liability for the same damage even if he or she acted lawfully. In the sense that damage could have occurred even if there was no illegal act, conditional causation is not recognized. However, South Korean theories and courts have provided strict standards for recognizing the defense of legitimate alternative acts.

The South Korean Supreme Court in a recent case held, "There was a possibility that the tortfeasor who caused damage by an act in violation of the law would choose a lawful act corresponding to the act. However, it must be determined whether the tortfeasor can claim immunity on the basis of circumstances that could have caused all or part of the same damage to the victim even if it was a legal act. In this case, the violated law does not have the main purpose of preventing damage, but requires strict observance of the procedure itself. Alternatively, if the victim's right to self-determination itself has an important meaning, it cannot be evaluated that the causation is denied or the illegality is excluded only by the probability of the tortfeasor's choice of legal action. In addition, even if it does not reach that level, whether or not the same damage caused by a legitimate act depends on the victim's decision-making or the action of a third party, such as permission from an administrative agency, itis highly probable that the same result will occur. Therefore, it is difficult to accept the defense of the tortfeasor unless it is clearly expected."[237]

177. As for the causation between the tortfeasor's actions and the damage, the victim bears the burden of proof. The degree of proof must prove a high degree of probability so that the judge can obtain certainty. However, in environmental pollution, medical malpractice, and product liability lawsuits, which are called modern lawsuits, in which the evidence for the proof of causation is ubiquitous on the tortfeasor, as introduced earlier, the degree of proof is alleviated by estimating the causation from certain indirect facts.[238]

237. Supreme Court Decision 2003Da9742 Decided Dec. 9, 2005; Supreme Court Decision 2005Da34797 Decided Sep. 21, 2007.

238. For environmental pollution, *see* Part III Ch. 4, paras. 141, 145. For medical malpractice, *see* Part I Ch. 2 §1 II. For product liability, *see* Part III Ch. 2, para. 134.

Part VI. Remedies

Chapter 1. General Principles

178. The Korean Civil Code stipulates general provisions on compensation for damages for breach of contract (Articles 393 through 399) and applies them *mutatis mutandis* in the Tort law (Article 763). In addition, individual laws on strict liability separately stipulate the scope and method of compensation for damages (e.g., Articles 7 and 13 of the Act on Liability for Environmental Damage and Relief Thereof).

179. South Korean tort law has recognized compensation for damages as a remedy for injured parties in principle and aims to compensate them. However, there is no definition provision for damage. However, theories and courts have understood damage as an involuntary loss of rights or legal interests. Therefore, it has been understood as the "difference between the hypothetical state that would have occurred without the tortious act and the current state caused by the tortious act" (difference theory). The purpose of South Korean damage compensation law is to compensate the actual damage suffered by the victim as a result of the offense. Therefore, in principle, punitive damage for the purpose of sanctioning the tortfeasor is not recognized.[239] However, in the case of compensation for non-economic damage, the principle of compensation for damages is monetary compensation (Articles 394 and 763 of the Korean Civil Code). However, when there is a separate regulation (e.g., Article 764 of the Korean Civil Code), appropriate measures may be taken to repair the injured party's situation.

180. Damage includes economic damage and non-property damage. In addition to active damage due to a decrease in existing property, passive damage (loss of lost profits) that could not have obtained a profit that could have been obtained is also a compensable loss. Regarding non-economic damages and lost profits, as opposed to economic damages and active damages, some countries have recognized liability for compensation in cases of intention or gross negligence of the tortfeasor. However, the Korean Civil Code does not treat the type of damage to be compensated differently depending on the degree of intention or negligence of the tortfeasor if he or she is liable for compensation. However, the degree of reproachability of the tortfeasor or the background of the harm is taken into account when calculating non-economic damage or determining the scope of damages.

239. In this regard, *see* General Introduction §3, para. 34.

181. Article 393 of the Korean Civil Code stipulates the extent to which compensation will be recognized among the damages continuously caused to the victim due to the offense. According to it, the compensation for damages arising from the nonperformance of an obligation shall be limited to ordinary damages (Article 393(1) of the Korean Civil Code). However, the obligor is responsible for reparation for damages that have arisen through special circumstances only if he had foreseen or could have foreseen such circumstances (Article 393(2) of the Korean Civil Code). In other words, ordinary damages, namely in the case of damage, can be generally recognized as causing the damage due to the inflicting act in light of the general rule of thumb in society. Compensation should be paid regardless of whether the tortfeasor is subjectively foreseeable. However, in the case of special damage in which the individual circumstances of the victim or the damaged object intervene in the occurrence or expansion of damage caused by any tortious act, the liability for compensation is recognized only when the subjective foreseeability of the tortfeasor of the special circumstances causing the damage is recognized.

The provision of Article 393 regarding nonperformance applies *mutatis mutandis* to tort liability (Article 763 of the Korean Civil Code). Therefore, whether the damage is ordinary damage or special damage is important in determining the scope of compensation for tortious acts. Distinguishing the two has not always been consistent. However, for example, in the case of loss of an object, the loss of value equivalent to the market value of the lost object is ordinary damage. Yet, lost profits from the commercial use of lost goods are generally treated as special damage.

In addition, in the case of infringement of property rights such as ownership, the value of the infringed property is ordinary damage. However, the non-economic damage suffered by the victim due to the infringement of property rights is regarded as special damage. The former ordinary damage is compensated regardless of the foreseeability of the tortfeasor according to the general occurrence of the damage caused by the tortious act. However, whether to compensate for the latter special damage is decided according to the foreseeability of the tortfeasor. Ultimately, it is determined normatively by comprehensively considering the circumstances and appearance of the infringement in individual cases and the contents of the infringed legal interests.[240]

For example, the Supreme Court of South Korea held, "If property rights are infringed due to the illegal acts of others, it should be considered that mental suffering is also recovered by compensation for the economic damage. Therefore, if there is non-economic damage that cannot be recovered only by compensation for economic damage, it is regarded as damage due to special circumstances. In an individual case, if it is recognized that the victim's building was severely damaged due to the underground excavation work, and it is recognized that he suffered serious mental suffering due to the shock and unrest in living life, it is judged that compensation should be made as special damage."[241] In addition, due to negligence in driving, it collided with utility poles and the power supply to the nearby area was

240. For determination on whether or not there is an adequate causation in South Korea, *see* Part V, para. 174.

241. Supreme Court Decision 90Da20206 Decided Jun. 11, 1991.

interrupted. As a result, the processing machinery in operation at the electricity-receiving plant stopped working, and the raw materials that were being processed had no choice but to be discarded. In this case, the Supreme Court of South Korea recognized the damage caused by the destruction of power poles and the subsequent destruction of raw materials as special damage. "The operation of the factory was abruptly stopped due to an unexpected and unexpected power supply interruption at the nearby victim's factory, which was being supplied with electricity through the telephone poles. The fact that active damage could result in the discarded materials is recognized only if the tortfeasor knew or should have known this."[242]

242. Supreme Court Decision 94Da5472 Decided Jan. 26, 1996.

Chapter 2. Kinds of Damages

§1. Individual and Collective Damage

182. The South Korean tort law does not distinguish between personal and collective damages in tort liability while maintaining the concept of remedy for personal damage. Therefore, even in the case of a mass tort or a collective tort that causes multiple victims, in principle, individual compensation by each victim is possible. However, in collective torts, damage remedy based on the concept of individual damages is not effective. Thus, recently, the collective damage remedy system has been discussed and introduced under the influence of the US and German class actions. Above all, the Securities-related Class Action Act was enacted in 2004, modeled on the class action in the United States. In a case of multiple persons in the course of buying or selling securities or other transactions, one or more of them may file a lawsuit seeking compensation for damages as a representative party with the permission of the court. In addition, when a business entity infringes directly on the rights and interests of consumers relating to their lives, bodies, or property, and the infringement continues, a consumer organization may file an action with a court to prohibit and suspend the infringement of consumers' rights and interests (Article 70 of the Framework Act on Consumers). Of course, consumer group litigation is limited to claims for prohibition of consumer rights violations. Although collective compensation for consumer damage has not been recognized, there have been active discussions on whether to introduce it.

§2. Direct and Indirect Damage

183. South Korean tort law distinguishes between direct and indirect damages. Direct damage is a disadvantage that occurs to the rights or interests of the victim due to the infringement of the rights and interests caused by the tortfeasor. Indirect damage refers to consequential disadvantages that follow other legal interests of the victim due to infringement of legal interests.

For example, in a case of personal injury, the victim's bodily harm and the resulting medical expenses are direct damages. Loss of income that does not generate income due to an injury is indirect damage. South Korean damage compensation law includes both direct and indirect damages within the scope of compensation. However, in case of indirect damage, among the infinite consequences that have a causation with the tortious act, it is treated as special damage in order to properly define its scope of compensation. Therefore, compensation can only be achieved when the tortfeasor has the foreseeability of special circumstances that cause such subsequent disadvantages.[243]

243. *See* Part VI Ch. 1, 181.

Meanwhile, the distinction between direct and indirect victims is also used. The former is the person who directly suffered damage as the counterpart to the infringement. The latter is a third party who suffers subsequent disadvantages through damage caused to the direct victim as a result of the infringement. The concept of an indirect victim is as follows. For example, the representative of the company caused damage to the company's property due to an illegal act on the job. As a result, the interests of the company's members, including shareholders, were consequently infringed. In this case, it has been used to support the rule of not accepting compensation for damages from members other than the organization itself.

However, this distinction is not necessarily clear. For example, a person who harms another person's life must pay non-economic damage to the victim's family and spouse (Article 752 of the Korean Civil Code). In the so-called power cable pole case, the factory facilities were shut down as the power supply was interrupted, causing the destruction of public utility poles. Consequently, for certain economic damage suffered by the factory owner, there is a possibility for him or her to recover it as special damage.

§3. Pecuniary and Non-pecuniary Losses

184. There is an opinion in which the distinction between economic damage and non-economic damage is based on the type of infringed legal interest. Thus, economic damage is damage caused to the legal interests of property. Also, non-economic damage is damage caused to non-economic legal interests such as life, body, freedom, and honor. However, majority views and precedents of South Korea distinguish between the two damages according to whether the disadvantage resulting from the infringement is economic or non-economic. According to these criteria, economic damage is a disadvantage to property. Non-economic damage means disadvantage to a person's mental well-being. In addition to economic damage, non-property damage can also occur in the infringement of property and legal interests. The same is true for infringement of non-economic legal interests. In relation to compensation for non-economic damage in South Korea, there is no such restriction, unlike in countries that only recognize it when stipulated by law. Article 751(1) of the Korean Civil Code stipulates that a person who has injured the person, liberty or fame of another or has inflicted any mental anguish to another person shall be liable to make compensation for damages arising therefrom. This provision is treated as a cautionary provision confirming that the damage to be compensated includes damage for pain and suffering. Compensation for non-economic damage is recognized even in the case of infringement of other legal interests such as name, portrait, privacy, etc. In South Korea, the liability for non-economic damage can be recognized as it is not limited to cases specified by law. Therefore, for example, in the case of "loss of enjoyment" due to the frustration of a planned trip, it is not necessarily regarded as economic damage. Even if it is treated as non-economic damage, there is no difficulty in acknowledging the liability for compensation.

185. Despite the possibility of compensation for non-economic damage in principle, it is not always necessary to compensate for the pain and suffering of the victim due to the infringement. For example, if economic and legal interests are infringed, it is sufficient if the resulting economic damage is compensated, and in principle, a claim for non-economic damage is not recognized. When there are special circumstances that would have caused the victim pain and suffering which could not be recovered through such compensation for economic damage alone, the compensation for non-economic damage can only be recognized when the tortfeasor knows or should have known these circumstances.[244]

In the case of economic damage, it is objectively determined by the market value of the infringed legal interest. Yet, in case of non-economic damage, determination at the discretion of the judge is inevitable. It is decided by taking into account various circumstances, such as the mental distress of the victim, the degree of injury, age, and living conditions, negligence and the degree of negligence of the tortfeasor.[245] South Korean precedents and the majority views of scholars have understood that economic and non-economic damage should be separately claimed as an independent lawsuit for each damage. Therefore, the victim must make a specific claim for each damage in terms of amount. The court must also determine the appropriateness of each claim by revealing the details.[246]

§4. Pure Economic Damage

186. Pure economic damage is a disadvantage that occurs in the victim's economic area without mediating the infringement of rights or legal interests such as life, body, personality, and ownership. There is the possibility of compensation for pure economic damage in the Korean tort law because Article 750 of the Korean Civil Code is the general provision on liability for torts. It does not make the violation of certain rights or interests a requirement for establishing responsibility for torts. Article 750 of the Korean Civil Code is historically intended to protect economic interests, such as business interests, by setting an open requirement of "by an unlawful act, intentionally or negligently."

This openness of tort protection against pure economic damage does not mean that tort liability must always be admitted for acts that cause pure economic damage. Business profits such as transactional relationships do not have concretely confirmed protections when compared with ownership. Also, it cannot be said that protection from infringement is always required in the light of the market principle

244. Supreme Court Decision 88Da27249 Decided Aug. 8, 1989, and many other Supreme case decisions.

245. There are difficulties in calculating such non-economic damages. Therefore, in order to rule out the arbitrariness of judges and to realize fair compensation between victims, non-economic damages is also determined by its index of tables in South Korea. As of 2015, KRW100 million in compensation for traffic accidents is set as the standard amount for calculating non-economic damages. In the case of injuries, the amount obtained by multiplying this standard amount by the rate of loss of operation capacity is calculated as non-economic damages.

246. Supreme Court Decision 88DaKa29269 Decided Oct. 24, 1989, and many other Supreme case decisions.

of free competition. Regarding the infringement of the claim of a third party who interferes in the business relationship of others, the Supreme Court of South Korea held as follows. "Although third party infringement may constitute tort, third party infringement is not always tortious. Depending on the aspect of claim infringement, it shall be determined in detail by examining whether it is established or not. It is insufficient to acknowledge the intention, negligence and illegality of a third party, when a third party simply knows the contents of the contract between the debtor and the creditor, and just enters into a contract that makes the contract breached between the debtor and the creditor. They are in a competitive contract relationship between independent economic entities. Accordingly, if there are special circumstances, such as a third party actively colluding with the debtor, or the third party using means contrary to to good morals and other social order such as deception or intimidation, or concluded a contract with the debtor with the intention of harming the creditor. Only in this regard, the intention, negligence and illegality of the third party must be acknowledged."[247]

§5. ACTUAL AND FUTURE DAMAGE (LOST PROFITS)

187. According to the Korean tort law, actual damage is caused by the loss or decrease of existing property to the victim due to tort (positive damage in South Korea). In addition, all future profits that could not be obtained in the future (passive damage or lost profits in South Korea) are regarded as damages to be compensated. However, in distinguishing the former from the latter, the actual damage is easy to prove in that it is a decrease in existing property. However, loss of profit is difficult to prove and complicated to calculate in that it is a possibility of future profit acquisition. Thus, the two are distinct in this respect. In addition, actual damage is treated as ordinary damage. However, lost profits, although not always, are treated as special damages and compensation may be limited depending on whether the tort damage is recognizable.

For example, in a case in which the victim suffered loss of profits that exceed the market price of the object as a result of illegal seizure, the South Korean Supreme Court held that loss of lost profits exceeding the market price is damage caused by special circumstances, and the tortfeasor is liable to compensate only if it is recognized that the tortfeasor knew or should have known such circumstances.[248] In case of loss of profit due to the death of an employee, when there are objective data that can predict with a considerable degree of certainty that the future wage income will increase, the future increase in wage income is also considered ordinary damage.[249] However, as the retirement age was extended due to the amendment of the Public Officials Act after the death of the public official, damages equivalent to lost profits

247. Supreme Court Decision 99DaKa38699 Decided May 8, 2001, and many other Supreme case decisions.
248. Supreme Court Decision 2002Da39616 Decided Jul. 25, 2003.
249. Supreme Court Decision 95Da29383 Decided Feb. 23, 1996, and many other Supreme case decisions.

due to the extended retirement age were treated as special damages.[250] South Korean courts have treated actual damages and future profits as separate lawsuits.[251]

§6. Other Costs

188. In principle, an injured party can claim compensation for expenses incurred for remedies of rights, such as cost in calculating his or her own damages due to a tortious act. For example, a victim who has been injured by a person's tortious act can claim compensation for expenses incurred in preparing and issuing a medical certificate necessary for a claim for damages.

In addition, the loss of physical examination costs due to personal damage can also be compensated by the tortfeasor. However, the cost of physical examination belongs to the costs of litigation. Therefore, according to the Civil Procedure Act of South Korea, the amount paid for lawsuit expenses can be reimbursed after the judgment is finalized after going through the procedure for determining the amount of litigation expenses on the basis of Costs of Civil Procedure Cost Act (Article 110 of Korean Civil Procedure Act). Therefore, in the case of physical examination costs, even if the party additionally spends expenses other than the appraisal fee fixed by the court, he or she cannot claim compensation by claiming it as a separate positive damage.[252]

189. For litigation, such as a claim for damages caused by a tortious act, the victim may be reimbursed for the attorney's fees paid by the parties by including the costs in the litigation costs (Article 109 of the Korean Civil Procedure Act). Attorney fees that victims can be reimbursed for are determined in accordance with certain rules set out in the "Rules on the Inclusion of Attorney Fees in Litigation Expenses." According to these rules, for example, if the value of a lawsuit is worth KRW 20 million, it is KRW 2 million; if it is KRW 50 million, it is KRW 4.4 million; and if it is KRW 100 million, the attorney's fees are set at KRW 7.4 million. There has been a dispute of opinions as to whether damages can be separately claimed for attorneys' fees, which exceed the amount included in litigation costs, according to "Rules on the Inclusion of Attorney Fees in Litigation Expenses." South Korean Supreme Court held as follows. "In determining the scope of compensation for damages caused by torts, it is not enough just that there is a natural or factual causal relationship between the tort and damages. There must be an ideological or legal causal relationship, that is, adequate causation. However, it cannot be recognized that there is a significant causal relationship between the tort itself that caused the claim for damages and the attorney's fees under the South Korean legal system, which does not adopt the law of compulsory lawyers. Therefore, attorney's fees cannot be included in claims for damages resulting from the tort

---

250. Supreme Court Decision 90Da18036 Decided May 24, 1991.
251. Supreme Court Decision 94Da16960 Decided Oct. 7, 1994.
252. Supreme Court Decision 86DaKa2200 Decided Jun. 9, 1987.

itself."[253] However, if the tortfeasor unjustly argues against the victim's claim for damages, thereby forming a new tort independent of the original tort, the attorney's fees paid for it may be claimed as compensation.[254]

§7. Mitigation of Damages

190. As introduced earlier, Article 396 of the Korean Civil Code provides for contributory negligence, and the amount of compensation for damages is reduced if the victim is at fault for the occurrence or expansion of damage caused by torts. This provision does not recognize a legal obligation to bring a lawsuit against the victim. Victims are given the responsibility to protect their own legal interests, and if they neglect to do so, they are to bear the consequences.

A victim's "negligence," considered a cause for negligence, means the victim's carelessness with respect to the occurrence or magnification of the damage. South Korean precedents have been controversial. However, in accordance with the purport of equitable sharing of damages, when with victim's negligence, the victim's causes, such as the victim's specific constitution, past medical history, and other physical conditions, are combined with the tortfeasor's actions to cause the occurrence or expansion of damage to the victim, the principle of contributory negligence is applied by analogy.[255]

191. Although there is no explicit provision in the Korean Civil Code, the set-off of profit and loss has been recognized. Therefore, if the victim has not only damages but also profits caused by a tortious act, the profits are deducted from the calculation of damages. The purpose of this is to restore the condition of the injured party that would have existed if the tortious act was not done to him or her. However, it comes from the idea that the tortious act should not make him or her better than it was before the tortious act. Whether or not profits to be deducted have occurred to the injured party must have a causal relationship with the tort. In addition, the deduction of profits must be consistent with the meaning and purpose of the liability for damages. In other words, even if it is a profit that has a causal relationship with the tortious act, deducting it should not result in unreasonable immunity from the tortfeasor. Therefore, for example, condolences paid by relatives in the event of the victim's death or insurance money paid to the victim through an insurance contract, etc., are not subject to deduction. However, when a worker injured due to an industrial accident has been paid disability compensation in accordance with the Labor Standards Act or the Industrial Accident Compensation Insurance Act, it is deducted from the victim's claim for damages against the tortfeasor to the extent of the amount received. The Public Officials Pension Act and the Military Pension Act provide deduction provisions for pensions of beneficiaries (Article 42 of the Public Officials Pension Act and Article 41 of the Military Pension Act).

253. Supreme Court Decision 78Da672 Decided Aug. 22, 1978; Supreme Court Decision 96Da27889 Decided Nov. 8, 1996.
254. Supreme Court Decision 80Da300 Decided Feb. 8, 1983. *See also* Part I Ch. 2 §3.
255. *See* Part IV Ch. 3.

Chapter 3. Assessment and Compensation of Damages

§1. Objective Versus Subjective

192. In case of economic damage due to the loss of an object, the victim may claim compensation for the amount of damage according to the ordinary value of the lost object. Ordinary value is a value that is generally accepted in a transaction and is calculated according to objective standards. It does not take into account the specific damage suffered by the victim due to the loss of the property. Victims can always claim compensation for damages according to their objective value, regardless of the foreknowledge (possibility) of the tortfeasor (Article 393(1) of the Korean Civil Code).

193. Even if the infringed object's subjective value to the victim is higher than the objective value, the victim can be compensated as special damage. Compensation for damage based on subjective value is recognized in that it should allow the victim to recover the state of property that would have existed if there had been no harm done through the tortious act.

However, according to the subjective circumstances of the victim, damage suffered beyond the objective value is treated as special damage in the Korean Civil Code. Therefore, if the tortfeasor knew or should have known such special circumstances, the injured party is entitled to compensation for the damages. When the damaged object has a special personal value to the victim, namely, the so-called victim's affection interests are not compensated in principle. However, a victim who has a special subjective preference or memory value for a lost item may seek compensation for non-economic damage as special damage.

§2. Concrete Versus Abstract

194. The damage to the victim is calculated according to the state of the disadvantage that has specifically occurred to him or her as a result of the tortious act. In other words, the damage to the victim is calculated concretely. However, the victim can choose to compensate for the damage according to the abstract calculation, for example, according to the objective value of the lost object, rather than the specific damage calculation.

Meanwhile, the amount of damage due to delay in payment is calculated according to the statutory interest rate[256] (unless the party stipulates otherwise) and is based on the abstract damage calculation method. When the victim claims compensation for monetary damages that exceed this delayed interest rate, Korean courts treat this as special damage and have held that if the tortfeasor knew or should have known of a special circumstance that would cause the victim to suffer damage beyond normal damage, compensation for the damage may be granted.[257]

256. Currently, the statutory interest rate is set at 5% per annum for civil cases (Art. 379 of the Korean Civil Code) and 6% per annum for commercial cases (Art. 54 of the Korean Commercial Code).
257. Supreme Court Decision 91Da25369 Decided Oct. 11, 1991.

In addition, even in the case of passive damage of lost profits, it is the loss of future profits that the victim could have obtained. Therefore, in this respect, an abstract calculation method based on the considerable probability of obtaining a profit has been recognized, unlike the positive damage of the current property loss.

§3. METHODS OF ASSESSING DAMAGES

195. The amount of damage is calculated when the object is lost or damaged, as described above. This is done objectively according to the market price or usage fee of the product. The starting point for the calculation is the time at which the tortious act was committed. Therefore, for example, when the buyer of a real property has suffered damages by purchasing it at a high price due to the fraudulent act of the seller, the buyer's damage is the difference between the market price and the purchase price at the time of purchasing the real property by fraud. After that, the case where the market price of the above real property rises above the purchase price is not taken into account in calculating the amount of damage.[258]

When there is a time gap between when the tortious act was committed and the result occurred, the tort must be considered complete when the outcome occurs. Thus, the point at which the tort was completed, namely, the point at which the damage occurred, is used as the standard point of time for calculating the amount of damage.[259]

196. As with the occurrence of damage, the injured party must assert and prove the amount of damage. Thus, the victim bears the burden of proof with respect to the facts that are the basis for the monetary evaluation of the violation of rights or legal interests. Concerning the degree of proof of the victim's damages, in the case of lost profits, it is necessary to reduce it compared to the degree of proof of the past fact that it is a decrease in existing assets in terms of future damage. Therefore, the South Korean courts have held that the injured party does not need to prove the concrete and certain income that he or she could realistically obtain but to prove the income that is highly probable within the scope of not losing rationality and objectivity.[260]

When it is recognized that damage has occurred caused by a tortious act, but it is difficult to prove the specific amount of damage in the case, South Korean courts have calculated the amount of damage by considering all indirect facts, such as the results of the evidence examination and the relationship between the parties revealed by the whole purpose of the pleadings, the tort and the circumstances in which the damage occurred, the nature of the damage and the circumstances after the occurrence of the damage. The Korean Civil Procedure Act accepts the rule of these precedents and stipulates as follows in Article 202-2. "Where it is admitted that damage has occurred, if it is considerably difficult to prove the specific amount of damages in light of the nature of the case, the court may fix as the amount of

258. Supreme Court Decision 2009Da91828 Decided Apr. 29, 2010.
259. Supreme Court Decision 2013Da65710 Decided Apr. 29, 2010.
260. Supreme Court Decision 85DaKa538 Decided Mar. 25, 1986.

damages an amount that is deemed reasonable taking into consideration all circumstances based on the entire purport of pleadings and the results of examination of evidence."

§4. Equitable Limitation of Damages

197. Article 765(1) of the Korean Civil Code provides that the person liable to make compensation may petition the court for a reduction in the amount of compensation, if the damages were caused neither intentionally nor by gross negligence, and such payments of compensation shall be a severe hardship to his livelihood. The purpose of this provision is to avoid the severe consequences of not being able to maintain even the minimum survival due to the fulfillment of the obligation to compensate if a person liable for compensation in difficult economic circumstances is liable for a large amount of compensation due to minor negligence.

However, if the duty of compensation of the person liable for compensation is reduced, the person entitled to claim compensation, who is the victim, will not be able to receive sufficient compensation for the damage. Therefore, it is understood that this article should be carefully and strictly applied. For this reason, it is difficult to find cases in which the claim for damage reduction under Article 765 has been recognized in the practice of the courts.

§5. Methods of Payment

I. Lump Sum

198. The Korean Civil Act, which in principle uses the method of monetary compensation, understands that lump-sum payment is the general method of payment. This is true not only in cases where loss or damage to goods is an issue but also in cases of personal injury such as death or injury.

Since the payment of a lump sum is the principle, it is necessary to relax the degree of evidence, such as acknowledging the death of a person, which is practically impossible. In addition, in that future profits such as lost profits will be paid as compensation for damages at once, deduction of intermediate profits has been recognized.

II. Annuities

199. The payment method of periodical payments is possible according to a special agreement between the parties (Article 725 of the Korean Civil Code). According to Article 751(2) of the Korean Civil Code, the court may order the payment of non-economic damages by periodical payments. However, questions are being raised as to whether the above provision regarding periodical money compensation for non-economic damages is legislatively appropriate because non-economic damage is not continuously repetitive damage for specific periods.

Also, there has been a question as to whether it is possible to order periodic money compensation in case of economic damage caused by bodily injury. In light of the supportive nature of periodical money compensation, it has been understood that a court can order periodical money compensation for economic damage (including both positive and passive damage) caused by bodily injury.

Even if periodic money compensation is possible, the victim can choose either lump sum compensation or periodical money compensation. However, the court is not bound by the injured party's choices. For example, "as in the case of vegetative humans, it is difficult to determine the duration of the sequelae of the disorder or the extent to which the remaining life expectancy has been shortened. Therefore, it can be recognized that compensation for damages by the lump-sum payment method may lead to remarkably unreasonable consequences in light of the idea of social justice and equity. Therefore, the court may order payment by periodical payment even if the victim requests for lump-sum payment."[261]

III. Others

200. In the Korean Civil Code, the principle of compensation for damages is monetary compensation. Exceptions to the principle of monetary compensation may be recognized when the parties express their intentions or there is a provision by law. Article 764 of the Korean Civil Code provides for special rules applicable to defamation. It provides, "The court may, on the application of the injured party, order the person who has defamed another's reputation to take measures appropriate for repairing the injured party's reputation, either in lieu of, or together with provision of compensation." This includes seeking measures such as cancelation or withdrawal of defamation claims, or disclosure of judgments regarding criminal punishment or payment of non-economic damage on the grounds of defamation. Advertisements of apology are no longer permitted due to the South Korean Constitutional Court's decision that they violate the South Korean Constitution. In addition to the Korean Civil Code, Article 77 of the Mining Industry Act, Article 131 of the Patent Act, Article 6 of Unfair Competition Prevention and Trade Secret Protection Act, and Article 14 of the Act on Liability for Environmental Damage and Relief Thereof stipulate the compensation method for recovery to the original state.

261. Supreme Court Decision 94Da30515 Decided Jun. 9, 1995.

Chapter 4. Person Injury and Death

§1. Pecuniary Losses

201. In the case of personal injury in which a person is killed or injured caused by a tortious act, the economic damage suffered by the victim is divided into positive damage, such as medical expenses and passive damage of lost profits. According to the difference theory, the victim's economic damage is a monetary evaluation of the difference between the victim's hypothetical status, which would have been the case if there had been no tortious act, and the actual property status caused by the tortious act (real damage theory or income loss theory).

Some scholars consider that in the case of personal injury, the victim's death or injury itself is damage (operating capacity theory or evaluation theory). However, if this approach is taken, the criteria for calculating the amount of compensation is not clear. Due to this problem, in practice, this approach has not been used. However, when it is difficult to calculate the amount of loss of lost income of the victim caused by a tortious act, the amount of damage is calculated according to the rate of loss of work ability based on the degree of injury. Thus, its calculation is reflected by the evaluation theory.

202. Positive damages to victims in the case of personal injury are usually medical expenses, medical device costs, and nursing care costs. In case of death, funeral expenses are covered. In addition to the previous medical treatment costs, the cost of future medical treatment is included if it is required continuously in the future. However, in South Korea, it is stipulated that nationals residing within Korea must be insured with health insurance (Article 5 of the National Health Insurance Act). Therefore, when the National Health Insurance Service has provided an insurance benefit to the insured because the grounds for the insurance benefit have arisen due to the act of a third party, the National Health Insurance Service shall have the right to claim compensation from the third party up to the amount of the expenses incurred for the benefit concerned. (Article 58 of the National Health Insurance Act).

If it is difficult for the victim to perform basic daily life on his or her own due to an injury, he or she can claim compensation for the cost of nursing care. Nursing care expenses also include past care expenses and, if necessary, future care expenses. In the case of previous nursing care expenses, it is assumed that actual nursing care has been received. However, when the victim receives care from a close relative without the assistance of a professional caregiver, even though the victim needs care, there is no actual expense for the nursing care. However, it is recognized that the loss equivalent to the nursing care expenses has been incurred. Funeral expenses are also recognized as the subject of compensation for damages caused by tortious acts. In practice, any expenses incurred are indistinguishable and compensated for a fixed amount.[262]

262. For adults, funeral expenses are accepted at around KRW 3 million.

203. Calculation of damage of lost profit caused by personal injury is inevitably more complicated than that of positive damage. The amount of income that the victim was not able to obtain, the degree of loss of work capacity, and the ability to operate are important factors in calculating lost profits. First, the amount of lost income of the victim should be calculated according to the difference between the actual income before and after the accident (operating capacity theory or evaluation theory). However, when it is difficult to actually calculate the actual difference in income, it is calculated by applying the loss rate of work capacity to the previous income (loss of mobility theory or the evaluation theory).[263] In this case, the victim's income is calculated based on the amount of income the victim was receiving at the time of the accident. If the increase in wage income can be predicted with considerable certainty in the future, it is regarded as ordinary damage and included in the scope of compensation.[264] In addition, in principle, the income of the victim is based on the income of the occupation the victim was engaged in at the time of the infringement. However, when it cannot be based on the amount of income at that time, such as in the case of trainees who are paid low wages before formal employment, it is calculated according to the estimated income that is likely to have been obtained depending on the victim's skills, qualifications, and educational background.[265]

If the victim earns the same income as before from work despite partially losing his or her ability to work as a result of the tortious act, such circumstances are not principally taken into account in calculating the damages due to partial loss of operating capacity.[266] In addition, even if the victim at the time of the accident was a housewife or had no income due to lack of a job, lost income was calculated based on the general daily wage.[267] Furthermore, when determining the amount of income in order to calculate the lost income of the victim, it has been an issue whether income tax (in the case of death, cost of living, etc.) is deducted. Although South Korean court decisions have been controversial, they have not deducted tax amounts such as income tax.[268] In the case of living expenses, in practice, about a third of the victim's income is deducted as living expenses.[269]

Second, the loss rate of work capacity is distinct from the medical disability rate in a strict sense. However, it must be calculated according to an objective method, not by the judge's discretion. Therefore, it has been generally based on the medical disability rate of the assessing doctor. Currently, the evaluation table developed by

263. Supreme Court Decision 85DaKa538 Decided Mar. 35, 1986; Supreme Court Decision 92Da19088 Decided Dec. 22, 1992.

264. Supreme Court Decision 88DaKa6761 Decided Dec. 26, 1989. For example, in the seniority-based pay system, wages are to be increased in accordance with the wage increase regulations, or promotion is highly probable, and this is the case. According to Korean precedent, when the retirement age is extended by the revision of the State Public Officials Act after the accident, damage equivalent to lost income for an extended period is special damage because it cannot be foreseen by the public. Supreme Court Decision 90Da18036 Decided May 24, 1991.

265. Supreme Court Decision 91Da27044 Decided Mar. 10, 1992.

266. Supreme Court Decision 90DaKa21022 Decided Nov. 23, 1990.

267. Supreme Court Decision 71Da467 Decided Apr. 30, 1971; Supreme Court Decision 91Da27044 Decided Mar. 10, 1992.

268. Supreme Court en banc Decision 78Da1491 Decided Feb. 13, 1979.

269. Supreme Court Decision 91Da8890 Decided Aug. 13, 1991.

McBride of the United States is mainly used as the standard table for disability determination. In addition, the evaluation table prepared by the American Medical Association (A.M.A.) and the rate table of loss of labor capacity in the Enforcement Decree of the State Compensation Act are also being used.

Furthermore, in order to calculate the amount of damages of lost profits, the operating period must be determined. In order to set the operating period, the life expectancy should be confirmed. In the practice of the courts, life expectancy is determined according to the "Simple Life Table of Koreans" regularly prepared by the Economic Planning Board.[270] In this case, the final decision is made in consideration of the degree of injury and its after effects. The operating period starts when a person reaches the age of majority, that is when he or she turns 19. The age at which the work capacity ends depends on the occupation in which the victim is engaged. However, in the case of urban manual labor workers, the age of 65 has been considered the end of the work capacity.[271]

Finally, if compensation for lost profits is paid in a lump sum, interim interest is deducted in order to prevent undue gain to the victim in that it is compensated for damage that may occur in the future at once. South Korean courts have used the Hoffmann method and the Leibniz method for deduction of the median interest in practice.[272]

204. When a victim dies due to a tortious act, in some countries, his or her family claims to compensate for the loss of the right to claim support suffered by the victim's death. However, in South Korea, the right to claim compensation for damage to life arises from the victim himself or herself and is passed on to the heir.[273]

§2. Non-pecuniary Losses

205. A direct victim whose life or body has been injured may claim compensation for non-economic damage resulting from it. However, Article 752 of the Korean Civil Code provides that:

> a person who has caused the death of another person shall be liable for damages to the lineal ascendants, lineal descendants, and the spouse, even where no economic damages exist as a result thereof. Furthermore, it has been understood that the protection legal interests (infringement of life) or the claimants set forth in the Article 752 of the Korean Civil Code are merely examples. Thus, the right to claim non-economic damage has been also recognized for common-law spouses, brothers and sisters, maternal grandparents. In addition, even in the case of an injury that is not a violation of life, the right to claim

270. As of 2020, the average life expectancy is 80.5 years for men and 86.5 years for women.
271. Supreme Court en banc Decision 2018Da248909 Decided Feb. 21, 2019.
272. When the future income is S, the interest rate is i, the number of years is n, and the present value is Sn, the Hoffmann method is Sn=S/(1+ni), whereas the Leibniz method is Sn=S/(1+i)n.
273. Supreme Court Decision 66Da1335 Decided Oct. 18, 1966.

non-economic damage from the close relatives of the victim has been recognized. Also, the right to claim non-economic damage is also recognized for infants who cannot feel the psychological pain caused by the damage at the time of the tortious act. The fetus also has the right to claim non-economic damage as it is considered to have already been born in relation to the claim for damage. (Article 762 of the Korean Civil Code).

206. The payment of non-economic damage is for the purpose of compensating for damage for pain and suffering. In this respect, it functions as compensation for damage, like compensation for economic damage. However, due to the payment of non-economic damage in addition to the function of compensating for damages, the victim obtains psychological satisfaction for the illegal act suffered by the tortfeasor (satisfactory function). The tortfeasor bears the obligation to pay non-economic damage, resulting in punishment for his or her illegal acts (sanctioning function). In addition, the payment of non-economic damage, which is unavoidable to be calculated at the discretion of the court due to the nature of non-economic damage, has a supplementary function (complementary function). Thus, when it is difficult to calculate the amount of economic damage, South Korean courts supplement it with non-economic damages.[274]

207. There are no provisions in the Korean Civil Code regarding the calculation criteria for non-economic damage. South Korean courts have held that judges should determine the amount of non-economic damage at their discretion in accordance with the purpose of equitable sharing of damages.[275] At this time, the judges shall determine it while considering not only the psychological suffering of the victim or close relatives but also various circumstances such as the degree of injury, age, occupation, living condition, negligence of the victim, the circumstances of the infringement, the degree of intention or negligence of the tortfeasor, and the state of the property.[276] However, in terms of legal stability regarding the payment of non-economic damage, in practice, the standard amount for calculating non-economic damage has been set at the meetings of the presiding judges in charge of compensation for traffic and industrial accidents at the Seoul Central District Court in order to promote the standardization of non-economic damage. In 2015, in case of death without the victim's negligence, KRW 100 million is the standard amount for calculation. In case of loss of work capacity caused by injury, it has been calculated as the amount obtained by multiplying the above standard amount by the loss rate of operating capacity. If the victim is at fault, the amount reduced by 60% of the victim's fault ratio from the above standard amount is determined as non-economic damage.

274. Supreme Court Decision 84DaKa722 Decided Nov. 13, 1984; Supreme Court Decision 2002Da53865 Decided Nov. 12, 2004.
275. Supreme Court Decision 847aKa57 Decided Feb. 8, 1988.
276. Supreme Court Decision 84DaKa722 Decided Nov. 13, 1984.

Chapter 5. Various Damages (Property)

208. In the case of economic damage to the victim, the Korean Civil Code seeks to pay compensation by evaluating the difference between the current state of property due to the tortious act and the hypothetic property that would have been without the tortious act. In the case of loss of things, the value is based on the exchange price of the things at the time of infringement. Regarding the loss of use profit that became unavailable due to the loss of things, the Supreme Court of South Korea recognized compensation only for the exchange price on the grounds that future use gains are included in the exchange value in case of total damage due to the loss of the things.[277] However, recently, in the case of loss of a business product due to a tortious act, damage from business suspension, which is expected to have been obtained if the product had been continuously operated for a reasonable period of time necessary to prepare another product to replace it, is also recognized as ordinary damage that should be compensated separately from the exchange value.[278]

209. In the case of damage to an object due to a tortious act, the amount of damage is the cost required to repair the object at the time of infringement as ordinary damage. Damage due to failure to use it for a considerable period of time required for repair is also considered ordinary damage due to infringement on the object. When some non-repairable parts remain after repairing a damaged item, the reduction in exchange value due to the inability to repair is also included in compensation.[279] Furthermore, a recent Supreme Court decision held, "It is technically possible to repair a car damaged in an automobile accident, so that the car can be used normally. However, in the case of an accident with serious damage due to the breakage of the main skeleton of the car, it is restored to its original state after completing all technically possible repairs. Yet, if unrepairable parts remain, damages caused by the drop in automobile prices are ordinary damages and must be compensated."[280]

§1. Insurance

210. Liability insurance, in which the insurer assumes the risk of loss due to the burden of liability for damages, has been widely used in South Korea as well. Professional liability insurance has been actively used by professionals such as doctors, lawyers, and certified public accountants to prepare for the burden of liability for damages caused by work-related negligence. In the case of companies, as the minority shareholder movement has been active, the number of executives' liability insurance has also been increasing to prepare for damages caused by executives' violation of their duties. In the case of individuals, the number of cases of daily life liability insurance to insure the liability for damages incurred by causing damage to

277. Supreme Court Decision 66Da1684 Decided Dec. 6, 1966.
278. Supreme Court en banc Decision 2001Da82507 Decided Mar. 18, 2004.
279. Supreme Court Decision 91Da28719 Decided Feb. 11, 1992.
280. Supreme Court Decision 2016Da248806 Decided May 17, 2007.

others in the course of daily life has been increasing. In addition to the above insurance for third parties, the risk of loss of the victim is assumed by insurance even through non-life insurance such as fire insurance and personal insurance such as accident insurance.

211. In addition to liability insurance that the insured voluntarily purchases, there are cases in which the purchase of liability insurance is compulsory by law. Above all, according to the Guarantee of Automobile Accident Compensation Act, any motor vehicle owner shall purchase a liability insurance policy or enter into a liability mutual aid agreement which covers an amount prescribed by Presidential Decree that shall be paid to a third party who has died or been injured due to the operation of the motor vehicle (Article 5 of Guarantee of Automobile Accident Compensation Act). In order to guarantee the payment of damages to the victim, the victim may file a claim for insurance money with the insurer so that such insurance money is directly paid to the victim. (Article 10(1) of the Guarantee of Automobile Accident Compensation Act). In addition, according to Article 5 of the Nuclear Liability Act and Article 17 of the Act on Liability for Environmental Damage And Relief, certain business operators must purchase liability insurance to guarantee liability for damages to others in the course of their business activities.

212. In case the victim has received insurance money from the non-life insurance that he or she has purchased due to an insurance accident caused by a third party, the insurer may subrogate the right of the victim to a third party within the limit of the amount paid (Article 682 of the Korean Commercial Code). In the case of accident insurance, if the party to the insurance contract agrees to subrogate the insurer, the insured's rights to a third party can only be subrogated to the extent that the rights of the insured are not impaired. In the Industrial Accident Compensation Insurance Act and the National Health Insurance Act, as introduced below, subrogation of insurers by the National Health Service that paid social security medical care benefits has been recognized.

§2. Social Security

213. The social security system, based on the idea that the social community should bear the liability for damages caused by torts, also plays an important role in tort liability. In the case of South Korea, first of all, the Industrial Accident Compensation Insurance Act and the National Health Insurance Act should be introduced. The purpose of the Industrial Accident Compensation Insurance Act is to protect employees by compensating them promptly and fairly for any occupational accident through the industrial accident compensation insurance business. And the purpose of the National Health Insurance Act is to improve citizens' health and promote social security by providing citizens with insurance benefits for the prevention, diagnosis, and medical treatment of and rehabilitation from diseases and injury, for childbirth and death, and for improvement of health.

214. The Industrial Accident Compensation Insurance Act was enacted in 1963 during the early industrialization process of South Korea. It has been implemented to promptly and fairly compensate workers for occupational accidents, and to promote rehabilitation and return injured workers to society. Regarding occupational accidents of workers, if Article 78 and its following provisions of the Labor Standards Act are occupational accidents, the employer is not questioned whether or not the employer is at fault. Therefore, as a disaster risk due to business activities of a company, the employer is obliged to pay a certain amount of compensation.

However, the employer's liability for compensation under the Labor Standards Act has a weakness in that the employer's liability is the basis for the liability property. Therefore, the Industrial Accident Compensation Insurance Act was enacted and operated as a social insurance system under the solidarity of business owners and national support. Industrial Accident Compensation Insurance is operated by the Korea Labor Welfare Corporation. Accident compensation under the Industrial Accident Compensation Insurance Act is subject to "occupational accidents," that is, cases where an injury, disease, disability, or death occurs due to an occupational accident or disease. Accidents while performing work, accidents due to defects in facilities, and accidents while commuting to and from work also fall under occupational accidents, such as those that occur while using the means of transportation provided by the business operator. Occupational diseases include diseases caused by harmful or risk factors and diseases caused by occupational injuries (Article 37 of the Industrial Accident Compensation Insurance Act).

215. The National Health Insurance Act is a law whose purpose is to contribute to the improvement of national health and social security by providing insurance benefits for the prevention, diagnosis, and treatment of diseases and injuries of people. According to this law, Korean nationals residing in South Korea become the insured of the health insurance based on the employee insured or self-employed insured (Articles 5 and 6 of the National Health Insurance Act). The insurer of health insurance is the National Health Insurance Corporation established by the state, which provides medical care benefits such as medical examination and examination, treatment and surgery, hospitalization and nursing care for diseases, injuries, childbirth, etc. of the insured and dependents (Article 41 of the National Health Insurance Act).

216. When the Social Service has provided an insurance benefit to the insured or dependent because the grounds for the insurance benefit have arisen due to the act of a third party, the Social Service shall have the right to claim compensation from the third party up to the amount of the expenses incurred for the benefit concerned (Article 87(1) of the Industrial Accident Compensation Insurance Act, Article 58(1) of the National Health Insurance Act). Where the person who receives the insurance benefit has already received compensation for the loss from the third party, the Social Service shall withhold the insurance benefit up to the amount of such compensation (Article 87(2) of the Industrial Accident Compensation Insurance Act, Article 58(2) of the National Health Insurance Act). The right to receive insurance benefits under these Acts is protected by making it impossible for them to be transferred or seized (Article 88 of the Industrial Accident Compensation Insurance Act, Article 59 of the National Health Insurance Act).

§3. Others

217. In the case of occupations or facilities that have a risk of causing damage to others in order to socialize damage caused by tortious acts, there are cases where mutual aid associations are operated to pay compensation for accidents. For example, in order to prevent school safety accidents and to promptly and appropriately compensate for the damage suffered by students and other participants in educational activities due to school safety accidents, the Act on the Prevention and Compensation of School Safety Accidents has been enacted and implemented.

Where benefits are paid in accordance with this Act for damage caused by school safety accidents, the mutual aid policyholders who are liable for compensation are exempted from liability within the scope of the benefit (Article 45(1) of the Act on the Prevention and Compensation of School Safety Accidents). Also, for example, the Licensed Real Estate Agents Act operates mutual aid projects to guarantee liability for damage compensation of practicing licensed real estate agents (Article 42 of the Licensed Real Estate Agents Act and Article 33 of the Enforcement Decree of the Licensed Real Estate Agents Act).

Chapter 6. Others Remedies

§1. Restitution for Unjust Enrichment

218. Article 741 of the Korean Civil Code stipulates unjust enrichment. It provides as follows.

Article 741 (Definition of Unjust Enrichment):

> A person who without any legal ground derives a benefit from the property or services of another and thereby causes loss to the latter shall be bound to return such benefit.

The obligation provision concerning unjust enrichment has been influenced by the German Civil Code. The obligation belongs to two categories: (1) despite the invalidity of the contract, one party voluntarily pays the other party; (2) infringement on the property or rights of another person and using it without legitimate authority. The person enriched in good faith is liable to return the amount that he still possesses of such benefits. A person enriched in bad faith shall return the benefits received by him together with interest, and if there has been any damage, he shall also be bound to make compensation (Article 748 of the Korean Civil Code).

Unlike the liability for compensation for damages caused by torts, restitution for unjust enrichment does not ask whether the beneficiary is intentional or negligent. The right to claim for damages resulting from an unlawful act shall lapse if not exercised within three years commencing from the date on which the injured party becomes aware of such damage and of the identity of the person who caused it. Also, the right to claim for damages shall lapse if ten years have elapsed from the time when the unlawful act was committed (Article 766 of the Korean Civil Code). However, the extinctive prescription of the right to claim for unjust enrichment shall become complete if not exercised for a period of ten years (Article 162 of the Korean Civil Code).

219. In South Korea, it has been debated whether or not it is possible to claim the offender to return all of the illegally obtained benefits as unjust enrichment in order to punish those who illegally infringe on the goods and rights of others. Some scholars have attempted to affirm the return of unjust enrichment by adapting the theory of "restitution in unjust enrichment by wrongs, restitution for wrongs" developed from the Anglo-American law in South Korea.

However, the majority of South Korean scholars have not interpreted the return of excess benefit due to the efforts or talents of the offender as the content of the obligation to return unjust enrichment. It is based on the ground that, even in the case of unjust enrichment that infringes on the goods or properties of others, the gains to the beneficiary must be due to the loss of the property of the loser.[281] However, there are exceptions to individual laws. For example, Article 43 of the Trust

281. Kim, Sang-Jung, *British Restitution for Wrongs and Return of Illegal Benefit*, The Journal of Korean Civil Law No. 78, 325, 2017.

Act stipulates that if a trustee violates certain obligations stipulated by the Trust Act, all benefits obtained by the trustee or a third party shall be returned to the trust property even if no damage has occurred to the trust property. In addition, Article 8(1) of the Act on the Regulation and Punishment of Criminal Proceeds Concealment, which is a criminal law, stipulates that criminal proceeds related to a specific crime committed for the purpose of acquiring illegal property benefits and the property derived therefrom may be confiscated.

§2. Injunctive Relief

220. In cases where liability for damages resulting from torts may be a problem, injunctive relief for injunctions to prevent torts in advance has widely been recognized in South Korea. For a request for an injunction, only the illegal act of infringing on the rights or interests of others is sufficient. Therefore, it does not require the intention or negligence of the actor, which is necessary to claim damages according to the principle of negligence.

221. In the Korean Civil Code, the claim for prohibition to prevent infringement of the rights of others is centered on ownership. Article 214 of the Korean Civil Code stipulates that an owner may demand the cessation of disturbance from a person who disturbs ownership and may demand either prevention of the disturbance or security for damages from the person who might disturb ownership. In addition to ownership, this provision is applied *mutatis mutandis* to other real rights such as superficies, *cheonsei* rights, and mortgages (Articles 290, 319, and 370 of the Korean Civil Code). In the case of defamation, the South Korean Supreme Court held, "By the nature of the right of personality, it is difficult to completely recover the damage and it is difficult to expect the effectiveness of compensation for damage only with remedies (such as monetary compensation or disposition for restoration of reputation) after it has been violated."[282]

Thus, by applying Article 214 of the Korean Civil Code by analogy, the request for prohibition of the violation of personality rights has been recognized. Requests for prohibition of illegal acts are also recognized in individual laws other than the Korean Civil Code. Article 123 of the Copyright Act, Article 126 of the Patent Act, and Articles 4 and 10 of the Unfair Competition Prevention and Trade Secret Protection Act stipulate a request for prohibition of infringement of rights or prohibition of illegal acts. However, violations of the above absolute rights or legal interests or cases beyond the cases separately stipulated by the law (e.g., recognition of a request for prohibition of illegal acts of infringement of others' competitive business activities) have been determined negatively.

282. Supreme Court Decision 93Da40614, 40621 Decided Apr. 12, 1996; Supreme Court Decision 2003Da1477 Decided Jan. 17, 2005.

§3. PUNITIVE DAMAGES

222. According to the difference theory, the Damage Compensation Law in South Korea, in principle, compensates the victim for actual damage. Therefore, like under-compensation, excessive compensation is not recognized. Therefore, the Korean Civil Code does not recognize punitive damages, in which more than the actual damage is paid to the victim for sanctions against the tortfeasor's illegal acts. However, in recent years, individual laws have stipulated that victims can receive compensation up to three times the actual damage due to the high possibility of reproachability of the infringement and the need to strengthen the guarantee of certain legal interests. Above all, there is Article 3 of the Product Liability Act, which states that if a manufacturer causes serious damage to life or body of a person as a result of not taking necessary measures against a defect of a product despite the manufacturer's knowledge of such defect, the manufacturer shall be liable up to three times the damage sustained by the person.

In addition, Article 35 of the Fair Transactions in Subcontracting Act, Article 13 of the Act on the Protection of Fixed-term and Part-time Employees, and Article 39 of the Personal Information Protection Act also fall under this category.

Selected Bibliography

§1. Tort Law in General

An, Choon Soo. *The legal Act for Another Person*, Torts, Unjust Enrichment, Torts, Management of Another's matters, Dong-bang Munwah-sa, 2018.

Eom, Dong-seop. *The Amendment of Tort La*w. The Journal of Korean Civil Law, No. 60, 2012.

Kim, Hyung-Bae, Kim Kyu-wan & Kim Myung-sook. *Lecture of Civil Law*. 15 ed., Shinjo-sa, 2016.Kim, Sang Joong. *Changes and Tasks of Tort Law and of Unjust Enrichment Law.* In *Changes and Prospects of the Korean Law in 70 Years (Professor Chunghan Kim's 30th The Memorial Dissertation)*, 2018.

Kim, Seong Tae. *Introduction of Torts.* In *The Commentary of Korean Civil Law [XVIII]*, 2005.

Ko, Seil. *Artificial Intelligence and Tort Liability Rules*. Chungnam Law Review, Vol. 29, No. 2, 2018.

Kwon, Youngjoon. *Theoretical Foundation of Tort Law and its Implications—On the Prevention and Recovery Paradigm*. Justice No. 109, 2009.

Lee, Yeon Kab. *Contents of Torts.* In *The Commentary of Korean Civil Code—Law of Obligations (6)*. Korean Justice Administration Society, 2022.

Park, Dong Jin. *Introduction of Torts.* In *The Commentary of Korean Civil Code—Law of Obligations (6)*. 2022.

Shin, Yu-Chul. *Development of Life Sciences and Civil Liability*. The Journal of Korean Civil Law, No. 22, 2002.

Suh, Kwang-Min. *Changes in Korean Tort Law and the Tasks of Tort Law*. Justice Vol. 32 No. 4, 1999.

Yang, Changsoo. *Changes and Possibilities of Tort Law.* In *Civil Case Study [XVI]*, 1993.

§2. "Liability for One" Own Acts

Choi, Heung Sub. *Pure Economic Loss of Tort Liability in Korean Law*. The Journal of Korean Civil Law, No. 71 (2015).

Choi, Heung Sub. *Requirements for Torts.* In *Development of Korean Civil Law Theory (II) (the 60th Anniversary Dissertation for Attorney Young Jun Lee)*, 1999.

Kim, Hyung-Bae. *Grounds for Attribution of Liability and Scope of Damage Compensation in Torts*. Korea University Law Administration Journal, Vol. 18, 1980.

Kim, Cheon-Su. *Medical Malpractice*. In *The Commentary of Korean Civil Code—Law of Obligations (6)*, 2022.
Kim, Cheon-Su. *Theory and Precedent of medical malpractice liability*. Daegu Law Review, No. 3, 2000.
Kim, Jae Hyung. *Infringement on Rights of Personality through the Internet.* In *Tasks and Prospects of Korean Civil Law in the 21st Century (the 60th Anniversary Dissertation for Professor Sang Hyeon Song)*, 2002.
Kim, Kyu Wan. *Basics of Claims in General Tort Liability Law*. Freedom and Responsibility in the Claims Law (the 60th Anniversary Dissertation for Professor Hyung-Bae Kim), 1994.
Kim, Sang Joong. *A Study of the Liability for Pure Economic Loss, Human Rights and Justice*, No. 328, 2003.
Kim, Yu-jin. *State Compensation Law*. In *The Commentary of Korean Civil Code—Law of Obligations (7)*, 2022.
Lee, Sang-Hoon. *Requirements for Torts*. In *The Commentary of Korean Civil Law [XVIII]*, 2005.
Paek, Kyoung-Il. *Defamation by Media reports*. Civil Case Study, Vol. 40, 2018.
Park, Dong Jin. *Duty of Care in torts*, The Journal of Comparative Private Law, Vol. 9 No. 2, 2002.
Suh, Kwang-Min. *A Study on the Attribution Structure of Torts*. Kwangwon University Press, 1988.
Yang, Changsoo. *Attorney's Faults and Responsibilities*. Civil Law Study, Vol. 6, 2007.

§3. Liability for Acts of Others

Cho, Kyu-chang. *Responsibility of Parental Authority for Illegal Acts of Minors*. Korea University Case Study Vol. 2, 1983.
Ha, Kyung-Hyo. *Disciplinary Trend and Legislative Direction on Restriction of Indemnity Rights in Employer's Responsibility*. Anam Law No. 40, 2013.
Je, Cheol Ung. *Critical Review on the Responsibilities of Legal Supervisors of Minors under Article 755 of the Civil Code*. Case Practice Study [XI], 2014.
Kim, Bong Su. *Legislative Theory of Employer's Responsibility in Civil Law.* In *Contract and Responsibility (the Retirement Anniversary Dissertation for Professor Kyung-Hyo Ha)*, 2017.
Kim, Hyung Seok. *A Study on Employer's Responsibility*. ParkYoungsa, 2013.
Ko, Seil. *Tort Liability of Possessor, Vendor and Lessor for Condition and Use of Land*. Anam Law Review, Vol. 47, 2015.
Lee, Jinki. *A Study of Civil Liability Law concerning Sports Facilities—Focusing on Liability of Possessor, Owner of Structure*. Sports and Law Vol. 17 No. 4, 2014.
Yoon, Seok-Chan. *Principle of Responsibility and Revision of Animal Occupants*. The Journal of Property Law, Vol. 28, No. 4, 2012.
Yoon, Yong Seok. *Liability for Damages Caused by Defects of Structures*. Busan Case Study, Vol. 10, 1999.

§4. Forms of Strict Liability

Ahn, Kyung Hee. *Analysis of the main contents of "the Act On Liability For Environmental Damage And Relief Thereof."* Civil Case Study [XXXIX], 2017.

Kim, Hyung-Bae. *Risk Responsibility Theory.* In *Retrospective and Prospect of Civil Law Jurisprudence*, 1993.

Kim, Chun-Ho. *Responsibility of Motor Vehicle Drivers.* In *The Commentary of Korean Civil Code—Law of Obligations (7)*, 2016.

Kim, Sang-Joong. *Current Status of Strict Liability and Legislative Discussion in Korea*. The Journal of Korean Civil Law, No. 57, 2011.

Lee, Hyeon-Jong. *Product Liability.* In *The Commentary of Korean Civil Code—Law of Obligations (7)*, 2016.

§5. Defenses and Exception Clauses

Ha, Kyung-Hyo. *Permissible Limits of Indemnification Agreement and Effect of Third Parties.* Kosh World, No. 41, No. 10, 1996.

Lim, Geon-Myeon. *Set-off of Profit and Loss*. Gyeongnam Law Review, Vol. 18, 2002.

Oh, Chong-Geun. *A Study on the Application Requirements for Comparative Negligence in Tort Law*. Ph.D. Dissertation of Seoul National University, 1995.

Song, Tuck-Soo. *Law of Obligations—Special Parts*. 6th ed., Parkyoungsa, 2023.

§6. Causation (Including Joint Torts)

Jeong, Tae Yun. *Requirements for Formation of Joint Torts and Aid by Negligence*. The Journal of Korean Civil Law, No. 20, 2001.

Kim, Sang-Jung. *Revision Direction and Contents of Article 760 of the Current Korean Civil Code Concerning Joint Torts*. The Journal of Korean Civil Law, No. 60, 2012.

Ko, Seil. *A Study on the Attribution and Apportionment of Joint Tortfeasors' Liability*. Korean Law Review, No. 74, 2014.

Ko, Seil. *Negligence and Causation in American Tort Law*. Anam Law No. 42, 2013.

Lee, Sang Chung. *Joint Torts*. In *Development of Korean Civil Law Theory (II) (the 60th Anniversary Dissertation for Attorney Young Jun Lee)*, 1999.

Lim, Geon-Myeon. *A Study on Hypothetical Causation*. Sungkyunkwan Law Review, Vol. 16 No. 2, 2004.

Yoon, Hyung-Ryeol. *Causation and Burden of Proof in Civil Liability*. Issues of Civil Trial, Vol. 22, 2013.

§7. Remedies

Jee, Won-Lim. *Scope of Damage Compensation.* In *The Commentary of Korean Civil Law [IX]*, 2005.

Kim, Sang-Joong. *A Study of Right to Request for Injunction as a Preliminary Remedy for Torts*. The Journal of Comparative Private Law, Vol. 17 No. 4, 2010.

Kim, Sang-Joong. *Liability for Damages and Prevention of Tortious Acts*. Juris, No. 43, 2018.

Selected Bibliography

Ko, Seil. *A Study of Foreseeability in Torts and Scope of Damages—Interpretation Problem of applied Article 393 Mutatis Muntandis by Article 763 of the Korean Civil Code*. The Journal of Korean Civil Law, No. 66, 2015.

Ko, Seil. *Discussions of Punitive Damages in the Civil Law Countries—A Perspective of Civil Law—Compensation in Continental Law*. Lawyers Association Journal, No. 63, No. 1, 2014.

Paek, Kyoung-Il. *A Critical Study on the Distribution of Proof and the Risk Domain Theory*. Case Practice Study [XI], 2014, 185.

Shin, Yu-cheol. *A Study of System of Damage Compensation Law—Focusing on Definition and Types of Damage*, Issues of Civil Trial, Vol. 23, 2015.

Shin Yu-cheol. *Massive Damage and Compensation for Damages*. The Journal of Korean Civil Law, No. 75, 2016.

Song, Oh-Sik. *Attributable Grounds to Torts and Theory of Preventive Effects*. Ph.D. Disseration of ChunNam University, 1994.

Yang, Sam-seung. *The Scope of Compensation for Tortious Acts*, Lawyers Association Journal, No. 49-2, 2000.

Index

The numbers here refer to paragraph numbers.

Index

www.ingramcontent.com/pod-product-compliance
Lightning Source LLC
Chambersburg PA
CBHW071346230926
51846CB00002B/462
9789403502793